Valparaiso Public Library
103 Jefferson Street
Valparaiso, IN 46383

IT TAKES
A SCHOOL

IT TAKES A SCHOOL

The Extraordinary Story of
an American School in
the World's #1 Failed State

JONATHAN STARR

HENRY HOLT AND COMPANY

NEW YORK

Henry Holt and Company
Publishers since 1866
175 Fifth Avenue
New York, New York 10010
www.henryholt.com

Henry Holt® and 🎟® are registered trademarks of Macmillan Publishing Group, LLC.

Library of Congress Cataloging-in-Publication Data is available upon request.

ISBN: 978-1-250-11346-7

Our books may be purchased in bulk for promotional, educational, or business use. Please
contact your local bookseller or the Macmillan Corporate and Premium Sales Department at
(800) 221-7945, extension 5442, or by e-mail at MacmillanSpecialMarkets@macmillan.com.

First Edition 2016

Designed by Meryl Sussman Levavi
Map by Gene Thorp
Printed in the United States of America

10 9 8 7 6 5 4 3 2 1

It Takes a School is dedicated to all the people who put Abaarso on their backs and carried it forward. And to three people who did that for me when I needed it most: Mom, Eli, and Billy, my original orphans and greatest mentors. Finally, to Orianna, may you always appreciate what a lucky start you've had to life, if for no other reason than because of your special mother.

To be without knowledge is to be without light.

—SOMALI PROVERB

CONTENTS

FOREWORD

Parts of the world, including many locations in the United States, desperately need high-quality institutions, be it in education, health, or other services. One of my goals in writing this book is to give readers a taste of the tenacity necessary to create such an institution. This work is not for everyone, but for the right person, it is a once-in-a-lifetime fulfilling experience.

The best way to describe the challenges we faced in building a school in Somaliland is to recount a few of the unexpected obstacles we confronted. While my situation in Somaliland is unique, the fact that we ran into trouble most likely is not. I expect tremendous difficulties will arise anytime someone seeks to create something meaningful where it doesn't currently exist. No matter where you go, such an endeavor will create misunderstandings, and opportunists who seek to benefit from those misunderstandings.

There are some people in this story who would prefer not to be identified, or whom I would prefer not to name. Accordingly, I've changed some names and identifying details, including the names of connected organizations.

One beauty of books is that they allow you to describe a story in great detail. This however is still limited by the reader's tolerance for just so many different characters and events. As such, *It Takes a School* focuses on a particular group of students I found most symbolic of the overall story. The group is predominantly from Abaarso's first class and I knew them the best since most were my advisees. We've had many wonderful young male and female students, some of whom have done as much or more than those described here, so my focus on these particular individuals is in no way meant to take away from the larger group. Likewise, I was only able to focus on a small number of teachers, staff members, and Abaarso supporters in the United States and Somaliland, but that too is just a reality of writing a book. This would be thousands of pages if I included everyone's contributions.

Finally, I am of course only human and my memory of the past eight years is imperfect. With that said, I've made this book as precise to the truth as I reasonably could. I've been through thousands of e-mails and documents, interviewed close to two dozen folks who shared the experience, and sent chapters as well as the whole manuscript to some of the major players for their comments. Fortunately, the vast majority of my experience occurred in either documentable form or with someone else present. I'm confident in saying that this book as a whole is very accurate in describing my experience in Somaliland.

IT TAKES
A SCHOOL

Somaliland and
Somalia in 2009

PROLOGUE

It is early summer 2011, near the end of our second year at the Abaarso School in Somaliland, Africa. The prolonged winter drought is well behind us, and the rainy season is in full effect, bringing with it the stacked pyramids of juicy watermelons and luscious mangoes for sale on the street corners of nearby Hargeisa. A good rainy season, when the desert blooms and the cattle get fatter, is always critical, but today the environment around me is little more than white noise to my mission at hand. My assistant headmaster has just ended our lengthy phone call with an alarming comment, delivered to me so casually that one might think it was a joke. Unfortunately, the absurdity we are dealing with is no comedy.

"Oh yeah, Jon," Harry Lee had blurted out, "I almost forgot to tell you, but there was a militia at the front gate. They came to kill you, but it's cool now."

Harry and I have a wonderful working relationship. He is a twenty-four-year-old American with a Chinese father and white mother, and when he had taken the position at this educational dream project of mine—an English-language boarding school in Somaliland—he had thought he was going to be teaching math courses and maybe organizing the school's basketball program. He quickly became my expert for just about everything—construction projects, water delivery schedules, program coordination, student life, and now security interface. He seems relaxed with telling me my life has been spared, probably because crisis management is our daily routine and in his mind this one is already behind us. If we are to succeed in this tiny breakaway republic, we have little time to waste. By all official definitions, Somaliland is still part of Somalia, but when a country has been in civil war for decades, national borders have little meaning, no matter what is "official." Somaliland operates like there is no Somalia.

I had been walking down a hallway of the main school building when Harry reached me on my mobile. We are always working and often coordinating, and I usually have to take phone calls on the move. Today's crisis, a gang of angry villagers climbing up to the school's gate in an old vehicle, isn't going to slow me down. I know who is behind it and I know he wants us Americans to leave, even though that would destroy the school. The indignation that I feel, that anyone would interfere with the education of these incredible, deserving children, is immediate. These interlopers haven't struck fear. They have drawn my fury.

It's not that I discount the risk and danger of being here. We regularly receive security alerts from the U.S. State Department and officials in the United Kingdom, including an urgent warning not long before this that a kidnapping was imminent. In fact, with the recent death of Osama bin Laden, foreign outposts are on highest alert, with retaliation being a huge possibility.

I have been working extremely hard at making the Abaarso School safe from attack. We have a perimeter wall and several guard towers, as well as a sizable security force. *Who* comprises the security team is in constant flux as we struggle to get it right. Some guards are described as SPUs, Special Protection Units; others are "watchmen." The SPUs are police units provided by the government. These guys are armed with AK-47s and have some training, but they have the distinct attitude of working for the government, not us, which they tell us every time we catch them "asleep" on the job. The private guards or "watchmen" are usually civilians from the village, and they do not carry weapons. In addition to the sizable disadvantage of being unarmed, such "security" is more likely to side with the villagers than the school in local disputes, and, in fact, the troublemakers at our gate include some of this former "security." Sometimes we have a combination of both kinds of security, but no matter what, the issue of loyalty is always part of the enthusiasm or lack thereof. There are usually eight to ten security personnel on duty, and thankfully, to date, there has not been any need to fire a weapon.

I am all too aware that serious harm or even death is a possibility. I am a non-Muslim, white American in a challenging landscape, which undoubtedly raises suspicions about my intentions. I am a target for many people—jihadists; those Somalia unionists against Somaliland's secession; fired employees; and even those who view my high-quality school as a threat to their for-profit schools. In 2003, a British couple, both of them educators who had taught in one part of Africa or another for thirty years, was assassinated on the compound of the SOS Sheikh School about one hundred miles east of here. They were gunned down by Islamic extremists who stormed their house as they were watching television in their living room. Two weeks prior to this, the same group had murdered an Italian humanitarian worker. Now there are very few foreigners in Somaliland, and those present rarely interact with locals outside of high-level meetings in offices and hotels. Foreigners are a target, and then here I come, a native New Englander with a vision for making something great, a restless urgency to accomplish it, and no tolerance for anyone or anything blocking my progress. The very fact of my presence, not to mention my style, has already made me some enemies.

Harry had handled today's showdown well. To their credit, the SPUs on duty did not let the gang of villagers in. As they all stood outside the gate talking, a student who had seen what was going on went to find Harry. As usual, Harry was brilliantly calm and controlled. First, he managed to find our head guard to ask him if the men had guns. No, no weapons, he was informed. Next, Harry peeked out the gate, where he saw a group of eight to ten men crouching in the hot sun, chewing the natural stimulant qat, which is widely used in East Africa.

The head guard spoke some English, so he could translate between Harry and the Somali-speaking band of intruders, which included Shamiis, the daft old lady from the village whose mouth was always green with qat. Harry's approach was to be as friendly as possible, hoping it would soften the aggression. One of the men said over and over that they had come to kill me, but they would settle for me leaving the country. Harry wasn't convinced they wanted to harm me, rather just threaten me. With recent events, he was pretty sure that the threat came from a personal enemy, not a more political group. Someone had put them up to this and he knew who it was. Harry concluded the group at the gate wasn't up for much confrontation, either; chances were they'd received some qat as a payment for creating this disturbance.

It turns out Harry read them right. When the school's call to *Al Asr* sounded, he gave them a way out by suggesting they meet again the following day, being pretty sure the group of villagers didn't want to interfere with a religious obligation. He told them he would relay their threat to me, but he personally didn't have the authority to make me leave the country or even come out now, and I was a stubborn guy, so I might be hard to convince. He was glad not to involve me, as I have a tendency to be righteous, which would only have escalated things and caused more harm than good. "Go back to your village and think about it," he advised them, and they motioned a retreat. Whether *Al Asr* was the reason or not, they piled into their van and left.

Those behind these threats have no idea who they are dealing with. My time in Somaliland has transformed me into my own brand of extremism. The school's success is my singular goal, and its failure my only fear. I rarely see my family, speak to friends, or think of anything else. Abaarso students have become my family, and their futures are now my reason for existence. I am never going to abandon Abaarso, not even with a threat on my life, because I can't conceive of life if Abaarso fails. I am already 100 percent in.

PART ONE

BURNING MY SHIPS

Don't look back. It is not where you're going.

—Anonymous

1

MY SOMALI UNCLE

My uncle Billeh's story began in the village of Erigavo, an old highlands town thirty-eight miles from the Gulf of Aden in what was then the British Protectorate of Somaliland. His given name was Yusuf, but, like many Somalis, he was rarely referred to by his given name. Rather, he was known by a meaningful casual name, in his case Billeh, Somali for "crescent moon." The crescent moon represented the new beginning of the lunar cycle, and a new beginning was how Billeh's mother viewed his arrival. She had given birth to a half-dozen daughters before she gave birth to her first son.

Billeh was one of his mother's nine children. His father had been in the Camel Corps, a legendary group of mounted police who kept order among the Somali clans on camelback. Billeh's mother was his fourth wife. In this Islamic patriarchal society, polygamy was widespread. The religion allowed for up to four wives simultaneously, although Billeh's father had only once been married to two women at the same time. There were advantages to an expansive family, as the number of wives a man had directly impacted the number of children, and children ultimately translated to a family's power. Billeh's father had fifteen children, who have multiplied to an extended family of more than two hundred.

Billeh was the first son to this wife, a revered position in Somali society. When he was born, clansmen came from far and wide to celebrate his birth, which, after six girls, was considered miraculous. Two more boys followed, but Billeh was the honored firstborn son.

Billeh did have a second part to his name—Osman—which was his father's first name. Nobody had a family name in the American sense. *Osman* told people which father he came from and the rest of his name comes from his paternal lineage. The limitation on the number of names depends purely on how far back one remembers. For example, I might say, "Mohamed is a tenacious little ball player." If someone asked me, "Mohamed who?" I could respond, "Mohamed Saeed." "Oh, you mean Mohamed Saeed Abokor, the one from Berbera." "No, I'm talking about Mohamed Saeed Abdulkadir Hashi." "Of course! Mohamed Saeed Abdulkadir Hashi Elmi Duale is a tenacious little ball player."

The longest name Billeh knew for himself was Yusuf Osman Abdi Mohamed Mohamud Ahmed Omer Deria Adan Mohamed Abulla Hamud Osman Saleh Musa Ismail Areh Said Garhagis Sheikh Isaaq Ben Ahmed. By Sheikh Isaaq we should be back six hundred years. Along the way, Billeh might have missed a few patriarchs, but he knew that somewhere around AD 1500, he came from Musa, who came from Ismail, who came from Yoonis, who came from Sheikh Isaaq. That's how he knew he was from the Musa Ismail clan, which is a subclan of the Habar Yoonis, which ultimately is a subclan of the Isaaq, one of the five original major Somali clan patriarchs.

In 1947, when Billeh was four, his father died, leaving his mother and all of her children to fend for themselves. He and his younger brother went to live with their eldest sister, who had a permanent house in Erigavo village. His mother and the other children settled at a little farm three miles outside of town, although, being nomads, they were often moving with the livestock. The following year, Billeh had his first go at education at a Quranic school for the youngest children in the area. These schools existed pretty much wherever there was a religious scholar willing to teach Arabic and the Quran, and Erigavo had a number of such schools.

The day Billeh's mother signed him up, she came in from the farm and took him to a park, where a group of children and their parents were lined up in front of a man who was seated on a small folding chair. Billeh's mother pointed to the children and told him that the man was an official from the government, and the reason he commanded such a crowd was he was offering the chance for an education. She said education brought with it respect and power, and Billeh would never regret being in school. She pushed him toward the end of the line, and the next thing he knew she was gone. He didn't see her again for a long time. But he still credits his mother who, with that one push, changed the direction of his life. He says if not for her, he would be a nomad today.

After the Quranic school, Billeh went to a small public elementary school that taught English, Arabic, and other subjects. Somali was not yet a written language, so it could not be a language of instruction. Classes were held in a tent, as there was no proper school building. There was a small tuition, which Billeh had to earn. He made money by selling *kidar*, a round flatbread about the size of a palm and made of sorghum. His sister would get up each morning at four a.m. to make it, and then Billeh would sell it at the coffee shop next door before going to school.

In this area, public schooling went only to third grade. The few children who wanted to continue their education had to choose from a handful of intermediate schools spread around the country, but far from Erigavo. Billeh took a standardized test administered to all third graders across the country and gained admission to the most respected school in Somaliland, Sheikh Intermediate School, a British-run boarding school for boys, where only the top scorers were admitted. After his acceptance, Billeh had to figure out how to physically get there and how to pay the private school tuition. The only way there from Erigavo was to hitch a ride on a truck following a desert track to Burao, then make his way forty miles northwest to Sheikh.

For tuition, his mother made a great sacrifice and sold some of her livestock. She diminished her herd of sheep for the sake of Billeh's education—it was that important to her. A first cousin of Billeh's, married to an English woman and living in Durham, England, sometimes sent him twenty pounds sterling to help with school fees. That's what Somali families did, they took care of each other. The clan support system was and still is the hallmark feature of Somali society.

The school had just opened when Billeh arrived. The teachers were former British army officers or Indian, a legacy of British colonial rule. After four years at the intermediate school, Billeh went to Sheikh Secondary School in the same town. With its elegant, two-story stone buildings in British colonial fashion, it was hailed as the most beautiful school from Berbera in Somaliland to Beitbridge in Zimbabwe, two thousand miles south. The headmaster, Mr. Richard R. Darlington, had been in Somaliland for years. He was a captain in the Somaliland battalion that saw action in Burma in World War II.

Billeh adored Mr. Darlington, who wore his glasses on the tip of his nose. The older kids didn't relate to him much, but Billeh saw him as a father figure, in part because Billeh had lost his own father and in part because he appreciated how Mr. Darlington prepared him for the world. Mr. Darlington taught the kids etiquette, such as how to use a fork and knife. Somalis didn't use utensils at home; everybody ate with their hands. Mr. Darlington wanted the students to know how to use silverware in case they went on to higher education outside the country.

Top graduates of the Sheikh Secondary School were being admitted to universities in England on full scholarships. However, during Billeh's third year, in 1960, Somaliland gained independence and the British left the country. Fortunately for Billeh and his classmates, USAID (United States Agency for International Development) stepped in and offered them scholarships to American colleges.

Thirteen students from Billeh's graduating class matriculated to American universities, and he was one of them. No kid from Sheikh School had ever gone to college in the United States, so this class had an extraordinary opportunity. Billeh had never been out of the country, let alone on a plane. The honor of being one of the chosen few was a huge deal in Erigavo. Billeh had gone from nomad to scholar and, in so doing, elevated the status of his mother, too. She was no longer viewed as simply a nomad; she was now the mother of an educated young man who had made it to the United States.

Billeh went first to Kent State in Ohio, then transferred to Boston University, where he met Marjorie Starr, an American woman from Worcester, Massachusetts. A contingency for his educational subsidy was that he return to Somalia after graduation to work for a year, which he did. He then returned to the United States to complete a master's degree in political science at Syracuse University. That's when he married Marjorie, who had a brother, Alan. Alan married a woman named Susan, who gave birth to me.

2

SOMALILAND ROOTS

Billeh and his family lived in Brooklyn, New York, and although I grew up in Worcester, Massachusetts, several hours away, our families were always together on holidays. He called me "Señor" for as long as I can remember, which even as a little kid made me feel special despite having no idea what it meant. I just knew he liked me by the way he said it, and that I was the only nephew with that title. In the summer, we'd often vacation with Billeh and his family, too. My mother and her sister-in-law, Marjorie, would rent various houses in different New England spots. In ninth grade, my parents got divorced, but the two women continued the tradition, even though my father no longer came. By my late teens, the rental was always a modest shared cottage in the Berkshire Mountains in western Massachusetts.

Back then, I could kick back and relax, so these were wonderful times. While I swam, canoed, and husked corn, Uncle Billeh would stand on the dock fishing for hours at a time. Sometimes I'd see him smiling as he fed fish out of his hand. At the end of the day, I'd realize that he never actually caught anything to keep. He was such a gentle soul that everything would be released, and for all I know he had bait but no hook, just feeding them by line. Nights would often be spent playing his favorite Somali card game, which quickly turned into my favorite, too. The game was complicated, bizarrely based on 187 points, and a player could be your ally one minute and your enemy the next. My mother's twin brother, Eli, often joined us, with the three of us locked in intense battles. At the end of one game, Eli complained that Billeh handed me the win with poor play. The complaint was fair—he had definitely handed me the game, which otherwise would have gone to Eli. But it wasn't poor play. I was family and a Somali man takes care of his family.

Everybody knew that Billeh worked for the United Nations, but we didn't actually know what he *did* there. When asked, he would say that he "deployed his experts to the field," but nobody had any idea who these experts were, what they did, or where this field was. I once went to a party for his promotion to a P5, but that didn't explain much, either, nor did Billeh help. "What does it mean to be a P5?" was answered by, "I'm no longer a P4 and am now one step below a D1." A Somali American who worked a mysterious job might sound like a CIA agent, but anyone who knew Billeh knew that this was not possible. He just led a quiet private life.

It wasn't until I was in my late teens that I learned more about Uncle Billeh's birth country. I was at a summer party in the Berkshires hosted by one of his UN colleagues, and the guests were talking about Somaliland. While the hostess knew it well, she and Billeh seemed to be the only two who did. Somaliland definitely needed explaining, even to those people worldly enough to know Somalia. Apparently, it held its own separate democratic elections, yet it was still considered an autonomous region in northwest Somalia. Billeh lamented that his peaceful country wasn't being recognized as an independent nation. Without this international recognition, Somaliland suffered economically, unable to secure international loans, have a seat at the trade table, or attract foreign private investment. This left the people in poverty and the education system in havoc. The days of potential scholars being prepared for global education were over. Someone like Billeh would not have access to proper schooling and would therefore be unable to launch to a university-level education overseas.

To those at the party, Somaliland's problem was as simple as having the wrong name. If Somaliland wanted to be considered separate from Somalia, a country defined by international media coverage of the Black

Hawk Down fiasco, which generated a book and a major motion picture, then you didn't use the same first six letters "S-O-M-A-L-I." It was hard to deny this branding issue, but I left that night with a different thought. Before the party, Billeh had been my gentle, intensely private uncle. Now that I saw how the hostess, Billeh's old colleague, looked at him and treated him, I viewed him in a new light. She had such great respect for Billeh and his potential role in improving his country's prospects that I saw him in greater depth, now recognizing this whole other "world-player" side to him.

In the following decade, while my personal career ambitions consumed my focus, my uncle's dreams for the people of Somaliland were never far away.

3

FROM HEDGE FUND
MANAGER TO HEADMASTER

On the outside, I looked nothing like a hedge fund manager. My wardrobe was from Target, and it wasn't that long ago that I replaced my used car, which was valued at less than my junior partner's Bugaboo baby stroller. I lived in Cambridge, Massachusetts, and even though my apartment was in a renovated Victorian not far from Harvard Square, it was a one-bedroom rental. I'm not denying, however, that it was a major upgrade from the basement apartment I had recently shared with a roommate, which had the entire building's plumbing alerting me when anyone flushed.

Before I was my own boss, I worked for a hedge fund in New York City. There was a dress code, and I did my best to comply, but I often took off my shoes and went barefoot in the office to be more comfortable. The bosses accommodated me because my ideas were also different, and they liked those. Once I had my own fund, I frequently went to the office in sweatpants and a T-shirt.

I became a hedge fund manager because I was highly ambitious and I loved analytical pursuits. I joined the investment world right out of college, knowing how much I enjoyed solving investment puzzles that required my brain. I looked at complex situations and then broke them down to their essence. Much of my childhood had been a quest for complexity—baseball stats, tactical video games, board games, and inventing my own entertainment because the board games weren't complicated enough. Before I'd entered college, I had created and marketed an analysis of the top high school basketball players in the country. Analyzing a player's prospects was an exercise in breaking down a series of complex factors. Naturally, I loved it.

I went to college at Emory University in Atlanta, Georgia, where I majored in economics and took a few finance and accounting classes at Emory's business school. Economic concepts came easily, and the finance concepts even more easily, so when a few internships introduced me to the world of banking and investments, I was completely sold. I'd get to use my brain analyzing the most complicated situations; the money would be a scorecard; and if I made enough, then maybe I could stop feeling pain at the prospect of splurging a dollar for a candy bar.

By twenty-seven, I was running my own investment firm, Flagg Street Capital, named for my beloved elementary school. I was in Stockholm, Sweden, talking to a room full of potential investors when one asked me, "You're bright and enterprising. What will you do when you get bored with this?" Such a question presumed a success I didn't at all take for granted, which perhaps threw me off. I answered without thinking. "I will help start a new country in Africa." This generated more laughter than dollars.

Now, at thirty-two, I was nowhere near as wealthy as my hedge fund friends, but my savings allowed plenty of opportunities for enjoying my life. By most standards I was a huge success, but in my judgment I was a failure. I'd expected to become one of the elite performers on Wall Street, the next Warren Buffett, but undeniably I was not. I had my clear strengths in analysis, but I also had weaknesses. Sometimes, I allowed emotions to infringe on decisions. The hedge fund industry was an ultracompetitive world of intellectual superstars, many of whom had and most likely would continue to surpass me. I had not become the best, and the money was no consolation.

I decided to close Flagg Street Capital, give back all our investors' money, and put my talents to a different use. The years since college had done nothing to lessen my ambition and ease my need to create something truly special.

How cliché is the story of the successful businessman who makes a lot of money, feels guilty, and suddenly grows a charitable heart? Well, that wasn't me in any respect. I didn't feel guilty; I was just unsatisfied with my meager accomplishments. Nor did I suddenly grow a heart. My mother had instilled in me a large one. For better or for worse, I was endowed with an often-painful weight of empathy. I've felt it for as long as I can remember, and I'm sure that's because it started in my early childhood. In fact, I trace it to the most influential events of my life, which actually took place before I was born.

My mother grew up in New Haven, Connecticut, with her two brothers as well as her parents, Ethel and Irving Dunn. Ethel was one of six children, along with Mae, Annie, Max, Henry, and Eva. While I would never meet any of them, they defined my childhood. In 1964, twelve years before I was born, Irving Dunn, her father, died of a heart attack. Four months later, my mother finished her piano recital to find that her mother, Ethel, had died while she was playing. Thus my mother was orphaned at sixteen.

In the years that followed, Mom's aunts and uncles died off in rapid succession. A story my mother told me when I was young summed it all up pretty well. Just a handful of years after being orphaned, she was studying at Clark University in Worcester, Massachusetts, the town where she would meet and eventually marry my father. She was at my father's house one night during their courtship when she was told her brother Bill was on the phone. She picked up the phone, terrified. Bill started the conversation with "Don't worry, it is only Uncle Max." Only Max! As in, this time it was only Max who died. He was an uncle whom my mother truly loved. But Bill wasn't being cruel. His saying, "It is only Max," was because he didn't want her to think that something had happened to their brother, Eli.

Then there were the letters. My mom wrote letters to my older sister, Beth, and to me, so if she suddenly died, we wouldn't be left without a good-bye from her. We wouldn't be fated to the sadness she still bore decades later after so many sudden deaths with no good-byes. Unfortunately, she told us about the letters when I was still very young. She believed if she were to die, these letters would be comforting. But I was a child, and this was a real miscalculation. I didn't want to think about a letter if she died, because that made me think about her dying. Even as a child I'm sure I saw that the letters were an expression of my mother's own pain.

To the young son who saw his mom cry for loved ones, the heartbreak of her losses caused a permanent scar that's still as sensitive as an open wound. I can barely stand to write the story even now. The world has so much death and loss and pain and sadness. At the same time, the world has people like my mother, who balanced her heartbreak with an optimism she shared with me and with others lucky enough to know her. She is driven by heart—damaged no doubt, but also 100 percent committed to live to her fullest, even if that means risking more pain. More than anything else, even in my youth I realized that my mother was vulnerable, people were vulnerable, and the more vulnerable, the more human they were to me. When I see their vulnerability, I project my own fears for them; I project their sadness.

With Flagg Street Capital closed down and nothing holding me back, I wanted a project that satisfied my ambition and engaged my empathy. Somaliland was never far from my mind; and in its postwar condition, it certainly needed help. So I called my uncle Billeh.

We decided to take a two-week trip to his homeland. There we met people he knew, and I committed to starting a great school to develop the future leaders of the country. It was an ambitious goal but also one in which I'd be helping children who desperately needed an opportunity.

It is not lost on me now that helping needy teenage kids, many of whom have suffered terrible tragedies, was an expression of the sad little boy in me trying to help his own orphaned mom.

4

MODERN-DAY NOMAD

Forty years after Billeh attended Sheikh Secondary School, and forty years after Somaliland gained independence from England and merged with Italian Somalia to form the Somali Democratic Republic, a boy named Mubarik Mohamoud was running away from his nomadic lifestyle and would soon enter my life. Many parts of the world had seen enormous progress, men had walked on the moon, and computers were now in nearly every American household, but the region where Mubarik lived had been static for centuries.

Mubarik rarely encountered people outside of his own nomadic tribe, so he knew nothing of progress. He was born in the Ogaden region of Ethiopia. While Ethiopian by name and national border, inhabitants of this territory consider themselves to be Somali, even if they've never set foot outside Ethiopia. He knew nothing about electricity, technology, or space exploration. He didn't know that Somalia went through a military coup and that Somaliland was now fighting to regain its independence. What he knew was herding.

By the time he was five, Mubarik was already shepherding the family's one hundred goats. His job was to graze the goats while keeping predators away. The idea was to run and shout at any animal that approached. When he got older, he was entrusted to graze the camels. He once had a close call with a cheetah, but when the encounter was over, he had scared the cheetah more than the cheetah had scared him. From sunrise till dark, he ran and jogged with the herd, developing a stamina for long-distance running, which would turn into a pastime. On the rare occasion that he saw a truck crossing the desert, he thought it was some kind of animal running quickly. He could hear it coming from miles away, and he could see people riding on it. He immediately assumed it must be some sort of high-speed camel. Camel . . . truck . . . same animal. *Why don't we have one of those?* he thought to himself. He'd see them only occasionally, and each sighting left him in awe. Eventually, he learned that these were man-made vehicles going places. He started to wonder *where* they were going and where else there was to go that he hadn't yet discovered.

When he was nine, word came from his grandmother that she needed help. She was living in a refugee camp, and the camp was counting family members present to determine how much food each would be rationed. The refugees had been living there for years, having been driven out of Hargeisa, the capital of Somaliland, during the civil war with Somalia. Thousands of people had been forced to flee Hargeisa, its residents relocating to the homes of relatives or to camps run by the United Nations and other humanitarian aid agencies.

Mubarik joined a hundred people to walk thirteen hours across the desert in order to boost his family's numbers. He had never seen this many people in the same place at the same time. Everybody, even the children, walked through the night, beginning at seven p.m. and arriving at eight a.m. the next day.

The refugee camp had a semipermanent look to it. There were tents, but there were also houses, traditional Somali structures of clay with thatched roofs. Mubarik stayed for about a week. There were kids about his age who, like his grandmother, had been forced out of Hargeisa. They were playing soccer, the first time he had ever seen the sport, and he wanted to join in. The kids started making fun of him, saying nomads were barbaric. He had no idea why they were insulting him like this, until his grandmother explained that these children attended school, something he knew nothing about. In fact, there was a school at the camp that went up to the fifth grade.

When Mubarik went back to his family, he told his parents that he wanted to go to school, too. His mother was sympathetic, but his father said no. No one in his family had ever been to school, and no one had anything good to say about getting an education. So his father thought he was a weak child because he didn't want to walk with the animals.

Mubarik was stubborn, and although it would be disrespectful, he thought it was necessary to defy his father. He told the family that if they didn't allow him to attend school, he was going to run away and never return. He didn't have a plan, but his mother, concerned that he would carry out his threat, convinced his father to let him study with a nearby community of Sufis. Sufis were Islamic mystics who taught Arabic and Islam in exchange for goats, a little money, a little food, anything a student might be able to offer.

Mubarik stayed with the Sufis for less than six months, which he counted by the moon. He didn't like it there; it was not the lifestyle he had in mind and not the kind of learning, either. Ever since he had seen the trucks crossing the desert, he had his mind set on learning how to build one. He wasn't going to go back to the nomadic life, so he ran away from his school and traveled to the spot where the refugee camp had been, hoping to find his grandmother. But the camp was now closed and his grandmother had returned to Hargeisa.

He found a truck leaving for the city and hid in the back. He had no idea that the ride to Hargeisa would be longer than an entire night and into the following day. Making it worse, he had been very sick and hungry even before the trip started. When the truck finally arrived in the city, Mubarik was discovered by the driver, who wondered where this ill child had come from. The driver asked his age, which he knew was ten or eleven, but he didn't know for sure because age was counted by the seasons, beginning in the spring. Every time the rains came, you just knew you were a year older. The driver wanted to help him find his grand-mother, fearing that he might collapse or die at any moment. It took days, but eventually they located her.

Mubarik's arrival in Hargeisa marked the first time he had been in a city, and it was overwhelming. Donkey carts rode down the middle of busy roads; goats ate garbage and wandered into traffic; chickens, baboons, wild dogs, and throngs of pedestrians rushed everywhere. Trucks, the rare wonders of his childhood, were now in the middle of congestion, overloaded with passengers and cargo.

Fascinating people filled Hargeisa's roads, including schoolchildren clearly identifiable by their uniforms. Mubarik didn't know where the schools were yet, but when he found his grandmother, he determined that his next stop would be school. He also couldn't believe the garbage. Where he came from, there were no manufactured products, so there was certainly no manufactured trash. Now everything reeked—the food, the exhaust, the open sewers, the burning garbage. Mubarik held his nose for three days, to very little avail.

The long-awaited reunion with his grandmother was gratifying, although she was very upset that he left his family and then stowed away to the city. Somehow, she got word to his father that Mubarik was with her, and of course he wanted to take his son home. Mubarik remained defiant. He told his father he would rather be homeless than be a nomad. The desire to go to school was his driving force, and with his grandmother's help, he managed to enroll in a private religious school in Hargeisa, taught in Arabic, which he found intellectually unfulfilling.

Mubarik stayed with his grandmother for about a year, until she became gravely ill and needed to move in with her daughter. Now he was essentially homeless. When he could, he stayed with people he knew, but he always felt like a parasite. He was often hungry and in the streets looking for food. He enrolled at a public school after he received permission from the principal. The curriculum was in Somali, so now he had to learn to read and write in that language. Whereas Arabic was read right to left, Somali was read left to right with a completely different alphabet, which was challenging, but Mubarik picked it up quickly.

In eighth grade, like all eighth graders, he took the national exam and scored high enough to qualify for the entry exam given by the SOS Sheikh School. Mr. Darlington had left Sheikh a couple years after Siad Barre's coup, and the school closed down altogether during the civil war. In 2000, SOS, a giant international nonprofit, renovated and reopened Sheikh and appended its name to it. At the time that Mubarik was in eighth grade, SOS Sheikh was once again considered the best school in the country. However, Mubarik didn't have the resources to attend SOS even if he was accepted, so he didn't want to take the exam. What good would it do if he wasn't able to go? But some of his school friends talked him into taking it with them.

The test was being administered in a nondescript public school building in downtown Hargeisa. Mubarik was curious to see if he could get in, although he was already feeling guilty. If he was to be accepted, would that mean he had taken the spot of someone else who might have had the means to go? What a position to be in. He had come so far, qualifying for the SOS Sheikh test, which meant he was one of the top students in the country. But whether accepted or not, he thought this opportunity wasn't going to work out for him. He was wrong.

5

RESULTS DAY

The day after the SOS Sheikh exam in September 2009, Mubarik
returns for the results, which are going to be read aloud at the same
school where the test had been administered. The examination board
had invited the top 150 students from the national exam, which had been
given in the spring. From this pool, SOS Sheikh is going to pick its incoming students. I had gotten permission to piggyback on this test to popu-
late my own incoming first class at Abaarso. We have been working on
the school for sixteen months and are finally ready to admit students.

Mubarik joins the crowd in the open-air courtyard at the center of the
building. He is with his friends, but many students have more significant
support teams with them—parents, siblings, grandparents, clansmen,
friends, even some principals and teachers from their schools. People
had traveled great distances from all over Somaliland to take this exam.
Those from Billeh's home city, Erigavo, had driven at least twelve hours,
much of them over harsh terrain one can barely call a road.

One young lady, named Amal Mohamed, had come from Burao,
Somaliland's second-biggest city, four hours away. With her for results
day are her primary school teachers and her best friend, Zaynab, who
has also taken the exam. Her mother had stayed back in Burao with

Amal's eight siblings, but Amal will call her as soon as she gets the results. She is looking forward to being accepted at SOS, a boarding school with a great reputation near her home. She wants to be close to her mother, brothers, and sisters.

Amal had been born to Somali parents in Saudi Arabia, where her father was working for the government. Her schooling was in Arabic and the family spoke Somali, so she grew up speaking both. She loved the sitcom *Friends*, which was broadcast in English with Arabic subtitles. She'd faithfully translate what was being said to what was written, and in this way she taught herself English, which she wanted to speak with an American accent. In 2004, her family returned to Somaliland. Amal didn't discover until they were at the airport and her father boarded a different flight that he was instead going to Ireland. She hadn't seen him since. He will be proud that she has taken the SOS exam, and she hopes she'll be able to deliver to him the same good news that she will be delivering to her mother.

One parent, Amran Abdi, has no student with her. She is the mother of Deqa Abdirahman. Amran has a college degree, rare for a Somali woman. A year earlier, she had graduated from Hargeisa University, having returned to college after raising her family as a working single mother. Deqa is not with her mother because she is boycotting results day.

Deqa had been outraged at her ranking on the national exam. She had finished eleventh overall, and while eleventh out of ten thousand should call for celebration, she was sickened by the unfair process. Through her teachers at school, she heard that bribing had skewed the results. She also heard that people had been buying the exam ahead of time. She knew she was better than some of the students ranked higher, and she was disgusted to have worked this hard and still not receive her due credit. She decided she wasn't going to go to high school, period. Education isn't mandatory in Somaliland, and a lot of kids, especially girls, don't go past intermediate school. The education system had turned off a great student.

Deqa's mother had convinced her to at least take the SOS exam, which she reluctantly had done. But she hasn't accompanied her mother for the results because, in her opinion, this test will be rigged, too. To be here in the crowd, her mother has taken off a few hours from her job at Somaliland's central bank to hear her daughter's fate.

SOS is taking only 50 students out of the 126 who have taken the exam, so tension is high. It is all a low-budget affair, no podium or microphone, just school and examination board officials standing on a raised porch with a crowd waiting below. Kids who know each other are chatting, but even then, the conversations are uneasy. *What if your friend gets in and you don't? What if you dash the hopes your parents have for you? What if you never have the chance to fulfill your dream of getting a decent education?* There is always public school, and there are other private schools, but this group is the best and brightest in the country, and SOS is in a league by itself.

Things quiet down suddenly when the head of Somaliland's examination board, a tall, amply bearded man named Daud, takes his place to read the list of students heading to SOS. One by one the names are read. With each name, cheers and whoops sound from wherever that child and his constituency stand. After a short time and many names, the sense of impending disappointment grows.

Amal starts to cry. *Oh God, please say my name,* she says to herself, clutching the hand of her friend, who is also still waiting.

Zaynab's name is called. "That finishes SOS," Daud says in conclusion. Amal's friend is the last person to get into SOS this year.

Mubarik's name isn't called, either, which doesn't give him relief like he thought it might. He doesn't know it, but he has just missed the cut for SOS by an alphabetical tiebreaker. The boy who is chosen ahead of him is named Mohamed Ahmed Abdi, whereas Mubarik is Mubarik Mohamed Mohamoud, so Mohamed Ahmed Abdi gets the final spot.

As for Deqa, her name hasn't been called, but her mother, Amran, doesn't mind at all. She is waiting for Daud to call out the next list, which names the students selected for Abaarso. Deqa's principal had been impressed by what he had heard about my new school and suggested that Amran and Deqa consider it seriously. Amran had even instructed Deqa to list Abaarso as her school of choice on the cover of her exam. Out of the 126 examinees, Deqa is one of only seventeen to do this. Most of the students have never even heard of my school.

By the time Daud calls out the Abaarso list, the excitement has faded. It is almost like the next list is for the leftovers, the booby prize. People are more bewildered than enthusiastic. Amran isn't; as she hoped, Deqa's name is on the list. Mubarik's and Amal's names are called, too, but they don't share Amran's thrill. Their first choice, SOS, is now full. They are directed to a classroom where they are to meet their new school's administration and find out enrollment details. Mubarik isn't sure he even wants to go in. Amal's reaction is even worse.

I am just about to enter the room to meet my new students when I see a round-faced teenage girl with black eyes sitting on the steps of the courtyard, crying hysterically. Even through her tears, Amal's spoken English is terrific. I want to know why she is so distraught.

"What's wrong?" I ask.

"I wanted SOS," she says. The way every Somali pronounces "SOS," it sounds like "sauce."

"Why?" I inquire.

"I just wanted SOS."

Grading the results the night before, I had seen that 87 percent of students had chosen SOS, and forty-four out of the top fifty. This was the first time I'd realized how revered SOS was in Somaliland thinking, in Amal's case apparently beyond even needing a reason. I know my Abaarso School will be better, but my business background should also have prepared me for how slowly consumer preferences change; brand loyalty is a very real thing. Amal hasn't told me that her best friend had been selected to SOS, both separating them and possibly creating jealousy.

I sit down next to her so as to be on her level, and I stare at her with a ferocious seriousness. My eyes are focused on this unhappy girl, who may never have seen green eyes before, nor ever had a man sitting next to her. "Look at me and listen to me," I tell her. "It just so happens that I'm extremely smart, and I'm going to make this school better than anything you can imagine. Your not getting into SOS will be the luckiest thing that ever happened to you. That's a promise." I may have been guilty of arrogance but not of misleading or overpromising. Indeed, I expected our results to blow away SOS. I fully intended to make sure of it.

I don't know what is going through her mind, but she gets up and we walk into the classroom together to join the thirty or so other students, most of whom had also wanted SOS over Abaarso. I will never hear a peep about "wanting SOS" from Amal again. The others in the room have no idea what they are even doing in here, but I have their attention. Step one to achieving my mission is getting them onboard, committing to enroll in a school they haven't chosen and don't know.

6

THE EXAM

Back up a couple of days to when the SOS entrance exam was being given. The exam had been created by SOS. My staff and I had come to the testing site to help proctor it, as Abaarso would also be accepting its students based on this test. Only about half of the 150 students who had qualified actually showed up. I couldn't imagine how this could be, when the national opinion of SOS was so high. How could some students travel from the far regions of the country and others not even bother to come? When the paltry turnout was confirmed, walk-ins were allowed to sit for the exam. I was baffled by how these walk-ins knew to be here. *Maybe this poor turnout happened every year*, I thought—which I soon learned was indeed the case. But how could random walk-ins possibly compete with the top students in the country? I guess the exam results would speak for themselves.

Those who had come were mostly boys. There were some girls, too, but the split was 85:15. Nor did SOS have the dorm space to take many girls. In Billeh's day, it was boys only, and while girls were now welcome there, they were a small minority.

Students would list their first choice—SOS or Abaarso—then after the scores were tallied, the top students would get their chosen school until one of the schools filled up. Then everyone left on the list went to the other. Foolishly, I thought we would fill up first. Boy, was I wrong. Local society was not aware of my dream to build a world-class school that would develop the future leaders of the country, nor would they have granted my idea any credibility had they been aware of it. My vision wasn't even credible to my friends back home.

I had a lot to learn about the ways a war-torn society is broken, and the exam itself would provide my first big lesson. The 126 students who were taking the test were spread over a handful of rooms. Each room was equipped with table-like desks, and each desk had a short bench, which jammed in three students. The kids were literally sitting shoulder to shoulder. In each room, there was a monitor from Abaarso and a monitor from SOS. Even then, proctoring so many students who were so closely packed together would not be easy.

No sooner had the test begun than the rampant and blatant cheating started. I had never seen anything like it. If you just walked into the testing room, you would assume a group project was in session, with the students beautifully joining forces to share notes and ideas. Of course, it wasn't a group project. It was a straight-up, independent examination with students engaging in the most overt cheating imaginable.

I decided that my best course of action would be to alert the SOS proctor in the room so we could tackle the situation together. He heard me, made one public announcement, and went back to acting totally oblivious. It was all on me, so I went around the room myself, personally taking on offenders. I warned them directly; I moved them around; I moved them apart—nothing was effective. The second I walked away, the students would go back to talking and sharing answers. If it were up to me, I would have kicked out half the class, but watching the way the SOS teacher responded, I realized it was *me* who hadn't gotten the memo. Cheating on exams was acceptable; punishing it wasn't.

At the break, I met up with my Abaarso staff and found they were already talking about the cheating. We were all North Americans used to silent exam rooms, and now we were one-upping each other for the most egregious act of cheating we'd witnessed.

As the exam came to an end, I decided to put dark dots on the papers of the handful of worst cheaters in the room, so I could evaluate their scores with this information in mind. Even cheating hadn't helped one kid. He had been one of the worst offenders in the room, leaning over for answers from someone else's test at every opportunity, but he had the fifth-lowest score of the entire group. In a way, I felt bad for him. He had been failed by his prior schools and should never have been put in this position. Three of the others hadn't stopped sharing with each other the entire test. Their scores weren't bad, and the best of them was among the top in the country, but how much had the cheating inflated his score?

Having scored the exams, I was able to answer my own question about how walk-ins could compete with the sixty students who showed up from those who had truly been invited, the "top" students in the country. It turns out that walk-ins absolutely could compete, partially because some of the "top" students in the country were obviously frauds. One of these scored only 21 points out of 150; eight others scored under 33 percent; and twenty of the sixty scored under 50 percent. Meanwhile, some of the walk-ins scored among the highest, earning six of the top twenty spots and nineteen of the top fifty. While there seemed to be some statistical significance to being a "top student" on the national exam, it was clearly limited. The idea that we were selecting from an already well-pruned elite was a myth.

Now, walking into the classroom where my charter class awaits, I need to win them over. That 87 percent of the students chose SOS over my school, including the majority now in this room, has my competitive juices flowing. I don't even know these kids yet; they are still just faces to me rather than real people. The only thing I do know is that they bet against my school. If I am honest with myself, at this moment, my desire to win trumps all other motives. It's not noble, but it is true. But, for me, my competitive streak has always been an asset.

Now that the kids are in the room, I give them a couple of examples of what will make our school different and exciting. I have my game face on as I walk up to the blackboard in the front of the class. There must have been an English-language class here before me because on the blackboard are English words and their negations using "non." There are a dozen examples and yet somehow every single one of them is wrong. Next to "true" is "nontrue" instead of "untrue," next to "able" is "nonable," and so on. Just by luck, one of them should be right, but none are. They are all "noncorrect."

English is an official language in Somaliland and there is a big societal push to improve citizens' proficiency, but success to date is extremely limited. There is good reason why Somalilanders should improve their English. It's estimated that only a bit more than ten million people in the world speak Somali. The language wasn't even standardized using the Latin alphabet until the 1970s. Accordingly, very few books are written in Somali. Without knowing an international language, Somalis will be severely limited in their academic aspirations. English is the key to unlocking education of all kinds.

"English itself is no better a language than Somali," I tell the students. "But English is the most internationally used language. I am just lucky to have been born in an English-speaking country, as it is the most useful language to know. You weren't as lucky, but with Abaarso you have highly educated teachers who are native English speakers." I then point to the board. "Every one of these is wrong. It isn't your teachers' fault that they don't know English; it isn't their language. You wouldn't want to learn Somali from me."

Of course, I am giving my speech in English to a mostly non-English-speaking crowd. That doesn't stop me from sharing enthusiasm, a universal language. From there I put some logic problems on the board, to be interactive and to show them another difference in our school. Abaarso will be all about challenging their brains to think, not memorize. I am heartened when the first boy comes up to the board to give it a try. Throughout, I keep my eye on Amal, who seems to be more accepting by the minute. I have no idea she called her mother and said, "Oh my God, I got into a school called Abaarso, and a white man teaches it. I didn't see *that* coming." She asked her mother what she should do, and her mother told her to give it a try.

Mubarik hasn't even wanted to come into the room. He has stayed outside so long that the room monitor at the door doesn't believe he has made the cut and wants to recheck his ID. Once inside, all he wants to do is run. He doesn't speak any English and has no idea what I am saying. He still feels guilty about not being able to pay, so he figures he is wasting everyone's time. He slips out of the room before the presentation is even over.

7

THE BLANK SHEET OF PAPER

This idea had been with me for a long time: to start a school for really talented kids who have great potential that will otherwise go wasted. Over a decade earlier, when I was still in college, I'd entertained the idea of finding the brightest inner-city children in America and providing them a great school where they could excel. I'd even dreamed up a business plan. The significant expense of this school was to be repaid by taking a percentage of the students' future income. This was the plan of an economics student looking to put the principles I was learning into action. I thought it was an investment beneficial to all sides. The students would know the school had every incentive to make them great because their success was required for its own survival. That it was probably "indentured servitude" and illegal was not relevant because I had just been an undergraduate tossing around ideas with my friends during a summer break.

The Abaarso School started as a blank sheet of paper I could fill in however I wanted. On the asset side, it had me, my starting donation of $500,000, more if necessary, and all my passion. That's really all I knew I could count on. Among the liabilities was my impatience. I was set on a September 2009 start, which was just sixteen months away from my decision to build it. As there were infinite directions that I could take a school—starting grade, size, students per class, background of teachers, boarding school versus day school, curriculum selection, just to name a few—I needed to choose one.

A favorite author of mine, John Irving, once said he couldn't begin any book until he knew the last line. From there, he worked backward to the last couple of paragraphs. He needed to know how the book sounded at the end so he could know how to get there. That's how I filled in my blank sheet. I started at the conclusion and worked backward.

Somehow, I already knew my last line. I wanted an institution that produced great future Somali leaders for decades and even centuries to come. I wasn't interested in a large school, and I wasn't interested in mediocre quality. Working backward, this meant developing all-around excellence of academics and character. Given what I'd seen and heard about the Somaliland universities, this could only be fully accomplished if my students were able to continue their education abroad. The long-lasting institution part of the plan also had implications. It meant financial sustainability and independence, meaning that the school could not rely on me forever. I had my last couple of paragraphs, and with that ending the rest of the plan would fall into place. I just needed to fill in my knowledge gaps so I could write it.

There are people who get PhDs in education and work for years before running a school. I had taken one undergraduate education class at Emory, which meant I had a lot to learn. Hopefully, I could accomplish this by talking to experts. I consulted with many individuals and groups, starting with someone I knew and then following his connections as far as I could. I had a professor friend at Boston College, Gil Manzon. Gil set me up with people there. Those people led me to people at other New England colleges, and then to talented teachers at New England high schools.

One day, I gathered a group of reputable science teachers to talk through all aspects of that curriculum. Other days, I talked to college admissions officers about how they look at admissions and financial aid for international students. All of these meetings filled in my knowledge base and ultimately helped me build the business plan. I was listening to their ideas and deciding which parts contributed to reaching my specific goals, and which were legitimate ideas but not for my school.

People would like to think that there are easy right and wrong answers about best practices in education. While there were no doubt some, I was realizing that the vast majority weren't so black-and-white, which was not to say that there weren't right answers for your situation. New Hampshire's Phillips Exeter Academy, a very prestigious prep school, had its own math curriculum that did not involve a single textbook. There weren't any explanations for how to solve problems, nor did the teacher start with an instructive lecture. Rather, students learned by taking on various problems that challenged them to discover the mathematical principles.

Such "discovery learning" was a wonderful way to understand the essence of math, and it developed critical thinking throughout. On the other hand, it took longer to cover material, required a motivated student, and could only be pulled off by an excellent teacher. It also was far easier in Phillips Exeter's small, twelve-students-per-class setting than it would be in a thirty-student-per-class public school. "Phillips Exeter Math" wasn't the right answer for every school, but it was the right answer for Phillips Exeter. I had to consider what approach would work best for us.

I loved the idea of discovery learning, particularly because future Somali leaders were going to need great critical thinking skills. My meeting with the science teachers stressed this point, as they noted the common conflict of pushing through more content versus understanding scientific concepts. These teachers were generally against the Advanced Placement tests in science, which they believed took the joy out of science. I took this point but also needed to balance it with my desire to send students abroad for college. APs were a way to prove their ability on an international exam.

While pedagogical planning was critical, I had many other things to do. During this time of preparation, I was reading my Somali language book, studying up on Islam, and communicating with Somalis I'd met on my trip, including one who promised to take care of all local issues. From these conversations, I was planning all of the nonacademic components critical to a school, from the daily menu to student life. Here I used my end goals to produce a general framework. First I asked, "Does this contribute to developing the future leaders of the country?" Then,

"What does this do to our finances?" One early conclusion from this was that our students would be eating a lot of beans.

In general, "bells and whistles," such as gourmet food, a fancy student center, and really nice dorms, would not contribute to creating future leaders. They did, however, most definitely create a financial burden, nixing them on both of my criteria. Private schools were often heavy on the perks and extravagant "curb appeal" facilities; even SOS Sheikh School had more expensive food than I was interested in offering.

My new students would not have those perks. Even if fancy dorms and a student center were free, I didn't want them, as I considered them more distracting than beneficial. Students should be spending time in the classroom, studying, doing extracurricular activities, playing sports, and performing community service. At the end of those activities, they could pass out in their pedestrian dorm rooms.

In the course of my investigations, I sifted through plenty of information that did not fit my end goals. I met with a woman at Harvard Business School who had been involved with the funding of schools in the Middle East. When I outlined my plan, she advised me that I was on the wrong track, saying that for $20,000, she could build a school and pay for five years of its operations. As I dug in, I realized that her financial model would essentially add another public school to the system, great for students trying to gain access to some education but impossible for the academic excellence I sought.

One clear direction was the need for highly educated teachers. I knew we needed them, but could we afford them? Finding such teachers would provide the first major challenge to my plan, pitting my goals of educational excellence and financial sustainability against each other.

The average salary for teachers in the United States was about $60,000 annually, which was completely untenable for my budget. After running various numbers, I decided that I could afford to pay only $3,000, which essentially made them volunteers at under $1/hour. In addition to this, I would cover their main expenses, flights, food, medical insurance, and housing, so the $3,000 could go toward paying down college loans or providing a little bit of savings. It wasn't a lot of money to offer, but it was necessary to keep our costs low so that we could maximize our impact and be financially sustainable. I was sacrificing, they'd be sacrificing, and we would expect the students to respect this and give us their all. My zero-dollar salary and the teachers' volunteer salaries would set the tone.

I didn't fully realize it at the time, but I had stumbled onto a "virtuous cycle" financial model, which directly contrasted with the "vicious cycle" of education costs occurring in the United States today. Many in the United States have heard about and possibly gone into a panic about the rapidly increasing costs of tuition. Many colleges are also in a panic, as they know they are becoming less and less affordable. Their answer, which has its logic, is to add all the features that help compete for full-paying students. That's why we see the five-star cafeterias, the environmentally conscious LEED certified buildings, the state-of-the-art gyms, and all the other amenities that didn't exist a few decades ago. Of course this all leads to higher costs, which once again push up the tuition rates. The answer of college administrators is to go after the full-paying students—and the vicious cycle runs again.

What I proposed was the opposite: pay very low salaries to keep the school's costs down and use the low costs to ensure that we get the most deserving students without worrying about their financial impact on the school. This will help the students and teachers excel, which will make it a satisfying job for teachers. Such a satisfying job means they'll continue to take low salaries. The model could be great if I could get just a handful of takers in the first year. And if I couldn't, well, then I figured I'd take fifteen students and teach every class myself.

There were many decisions colored by financial constraints, and I was quickly getting the sense that financially I was mostly going to be on my own for a while. At this point, potential donors just weren't believers. I thought I could run the school for under $2,000 per student per year, which was off-the-charts low when compared to high-end international schools, but even at this low price I couldn't imagine that the school could ever break even from tuition. Even a few hundred dollars per child was a lot for a Somali family to afford, especially since Somali families had many children.

Monetary considerations were the main reason I decided to start in ninth grade. From the standpoint of developing future leaders, I would have preferred to start younger, but I knew it would take until our students reached twelfth grade before I could show convincing results. To my knowledge, no Somaliland or Somali citizen had gotten a scholarship to a U.S. college since the '80s. Every donor was a skeptic now, but I was betting that that would all change once the first Abaarso student stepped off the plane in America.

PART TWO

BUILDING A SCHOOL

*Don't set about your journey using
someone else's donkey.*

—SOMALI PROVERB

8

FIRST TRIP TO SOMALILAND

The road to the test day had been long but energizing. On April 15, 2008, I boarded a plane at Logan International Airport for my first trip to a developing country. Just getting to Somaliland was daunting. It took more than thirty hours to get to Hargeisa, the capital. My flight had three legs—Boston to D.C.; D.C. to Addis Ababa, Ethiopia; and finally an eighty-minute flight by prop plane to Hargeisa.

Nothing in the books I'd read could fully prepare me for this extraordinary place. As my plane flew along the route to my final destination, I stared out the window like an excited kid. The landscape near the Somaliland-Ethiopia border was rocky and completely barren. It had been the site of the Ogaden War, also known as the Ethio-Somali War, when Somalia had invaded Ethiopia to reclaim territories they believed to be theirs, resulting from a classic African issue in which the Ogaden people were ethnically Somali but the European-drawn lines placed their region in Ethiopia. But from the air, the geography looked pretty desolate to me. I wondered what it was about this inhospitable stretch of desert that had been worth fighting for. Of course, things weren't that simple. It wasn't about the land itself, it was about Somali nationalism and artificial borders, both of which I would learn much more about the longer I stayed in the country.

The plane came down to a bumpy landing along a runway edged with a few similar prop planes, mostly looking like they'd been abandoned decades before. The small airport had no Jetways, just metal stairs that were pushed up to the aircraft for our exit onto the tarmac. Climbing down the stairs, I was immediately impressed by how little humidity there was, having always imagined Africa as a hot, humid place. Instead, there was only a warm, gentle breeze and bright sunlight. I was met on the tarmac by my own private greeting committee—Uncle Billeh, who had arrived a couple of days earlier, and a tall, well-dressed Somaliland gentleman I had never seen before.

On the car ride into the city, my uncle's companion was talking to me in a familiar way and we were getting along well, but Billeh still hadn't introduced us. Billeh was such a quiet guy, he probably didn't even realize he needed to. "Who is this guy?" I finally asked Billeh in a whisper.

We will call the man Khadar Ali, and he held a PhD from a top-20 university in the United States. He'd been copied on some previous e-mails I'd exchanged with Billeh about my trip. My uncle knew him from a couple of international conferences the two had attended over the years in Washington, D.C. When Billeh told him why I was coming to Somaliland, he had asked if he could join us, saying he might be able to help with my quest.

The road into Hargeisa was filled with billboards, mostly advertising the country's big telecommunication and money transfer companies, but the one that caught my attention was for a nonprofit organization that cleared land mines. It was a startling reminder that I was in a different world with some very different priorities.

Getting into the city was painfully slow. The roads were terrible and pocked with potholes and obstacles—cars, trucks, stray animals, and hordes of pedestrians both in the streets and along the narrow dirt shoulder. Also on Hargeisa's roads were lots of schoolchildren clearly identifiable by their uniforms, with some of the girls covering their faces with a *niqab*. All the women were covered to an extent I had never seen before. The men mostly wore T-shirts and long pants, but some wore traditional Somali men's skirts, similar to sarongs, called *mawiis*. What really struck me, though, was that grown men, some elderly, walked down the street together holding hands with interlocking fingers. No, they were not openly homosexual; homosexuality is prohibited in Somaliland. Somali men are just extremely comfortable with each other physically. I'd soon find that a Somali who shook your hand would still be holding it a minute later.

To add to the chaos, steering wheels were on the right in the fashion of British cars, but traffic also stayed to the right, unlike in England. This meant drivers in both directions were on the outside of the vehicle, making for harrowing situations and lots of accidents. At one point, we passed a donkey pulling a small wagon with a tank of water. The man seated atop the tank was selling water to anyone who needed it.

Water was scarce in Somaliland, and even in Hargeisa many households didn't have access to public water. This year, the lack of rainfall was causing great anxiety. By this time, the rains should have come, and every day they didn't caused suffering and worry. Somalilanders were desert people who depended on the rains of April and May to survive and thrive. Without them, animals and people would undoubtedly die.

Something else impressed me on the drive into town: how much trash there was. It was everywhere. Littering was a way of life. If somebody was drinking a Coke, he would just throw the bottle wherever he finished it. Thousands of thin one-use plastic grocery bags of every color were blowing around in the wind until they finally caught on prickly bushes and trees. They were so commonplace that only a newcomer like me would even notice them. People sometimes referred to them as "Hargeisa flowers"—not that the city smelled like flowers. Without factories, Hargeisa lacked an industrial scent, but certain spots offered the distinct smell of burning garbage. Some of those trashed Coke bottles were now wafting through the air as acrid smoke.

In town, my uncle and I were staying at the Maansoor Hotel, well located and *the* place to network with important Somalis and international travelers and visitors. From this home base, I would spend the next two weeks venturing out into the city and to other places within driving distance. I had a rough plan of visiting hospitals, schools, an orphanage, and the port at Berbera, a coastal city in the north, all with the purpose of better understanding the country. Billeh was often unable to join me on these "scouting" trips. Even on day one, he was already stuck at the hotel for personal/family/clan "business." Somalis are famous for their oral society, and someone had caught wind of Billeh's arrival in-country and his presence at the Maansoor almost before he had gotten off the plane. With that, the news went completely viral, as in Somali viral, to anyone and everyone even tangentially related to him.

"Relatives" has a different meaning in a clan society, which defines Somaliland. It was the Musa Ismails, Billeh's subclan, who knew that he was back in the country, and they wanted to see him. One will hear that "clan is everything" in Somaliland. Although this is a strange concept to Westerners, the clan is the cornerstone of social obligation in Somali society.

Each morning, Billeh would go to the lobby to find a line of "relatives" patiently waiting to see him. Clanspeople helped each other and expected money if one had it and another did not. Billeh would often tell me that the flight and hotel were only a small fraction of the final cost of his trips back to his homeland. His relatives viewed him as having enough wealth to share with those in need, similar to how he benefited from clan generosity when he was younger. Even now, he was getting something in return. The clanism worked in both directions, and although Billeh was no doubt a net payer in the system, a clansman of Billeh's had his car and driver stationed in the Maansoor parking lot every morning for our entire trip. His only purpose was to serve Billeh if needed.

At that time, I had no understanding of Somali clan "pressure," for lack of a better word. The clan and clan loyalty are the heart of any social, judicial, financial, or legislative decision. In some respects, it is a much broader view of family and family responsibility. In Somaliland, clan is family, and just as a Westerner is expected to side with his family, a Somali is expected to go with his clansmen. I had no idea in those early days how crucial an understanding of this system would be to my school's survival.

I'd arranged a guide for my trip who would take me around while Billeh was tied up at the hotel. She was the niece of a Somali woman named Edna Adan, who was world-known for her philanthropic work in Somaliland and a friend of Billeh's, and she generously showed me around the country. I would also come to rely on Khadar, whose presence was a pleasant surprise. His English was flawless, he was highly educated, and his activities in Somaliland included controlling a newspaper. He was primed to take me around, and he seemed to know everyone in the country. In fact, he told me that he had recently been a presidential candidate before being pushed out by corruption within his party. Khadar was married to an American woman who worked for the U.S. government, and he'd lived in the United States for decades, so he also understood my world. He had his own agenda for my trip, which, given my lack of direction, could prove beneficial.

I told Khadar that I wanted to build a great school for the most promising students in the country. He told me he knew the perfect place we could get land to build it. His enthusiasm was encouraging, as was his confidence that he could help. There was a location not far from Hargeisa that he would show me.

The next day, we drove to a village about twelve miles west of the outer edge of Hargeisa's urban sprawl. It was amazing how quickly we moved from city to absolutely nothing. First, we were driving along on the road, seeing buildings on both sides of us. Then, suddenly, all around us was empty space. There were open plains of emptiness, hills of emptiness, and mountains of emptiness. It was all empty. The land was rock hard and barren, and anything that should have been alive looked dead due to the delayed rains. Again, the condition of the road was atrocious, and the car lurched through one pothole after another. I couldn't understand why we were still driving. We'd already passed enough land to build a million schools.

In the middle of the nothingness, there was a makeshift security checkpoint, which consisted of a rope that was tied to two poles on either side of the road, manned by some armed security folks. While we were waiting for clearance, we were approached by women with baskets of fruit for sale, mangoes, guavas, and oranges that were still green. Apparently, their business was selling to cars stopped at the checkpoint. There were a few permanent-looking buildings made of concrete in the area, as well as a few buildings that looked quite temporary and a number of nomadic cloth huts. This, I was told, was Abaarso Village.

Khadar instructed his driver to stop the vehicle near a group of men standing by the side of the road. These guys were going to take us to the site Khadar had in mind. I couldn't understand what they were saying because the conversation was all in Somali. But after a short time, a couple of the men climbed into the way back of the car and started directing us where to go. We turned off the main "highway" onto dirt roads, which were sometimes just unimproved paths across the dry desert. After about a mile, we stopped and got out. The ground was incredibly rocky, covered with loose stones about the size of baseballs, often on top of large boulders pushing out of the earth. You needed to watch every step to avoid twisting an ankle. Aside from a handful of acacia trees, nothing was alive.

I couldn't figure out why we would come to this spot rather than any other place in the previous eleven miles of desolate land we had passed getting to Abaarso. To Khadar, it made perfect sense. This was a great place to build the boarding school and these gentlemen in the car were going to be generous enough to donate the land. Apparently, they had told him, "Our father never did anything with this land, so it just sat here doing nothing. We don't want to be the same way."

So here we were in Abaarso, on this empty hill with some rocks and dirt, and these people in the village saying it could be ours. I didn't even know whether it was their land to give away. They said they'd mark the boundaries with stones, and those were certainly in supply. I trusted Billeh, and he seemed to trust Khadar, and Khadar seemed to think this was not only legitimate but also a great opportunity. He had the résumé and knew Somaliland much better than my uncle, who had been in America for decades and had never lived in Hargeisa. The land did not seem like much of a gift considering land was pretty much in infinite supply, but Khadar said it was the right land. It was completely dry but he said we could drill for water. At the time I didn't know that *abaar* is the Somali word for "drought."

Several days later, we returned with some friends of Khadar's who he said would be helpful to our school. For all I knew, it may or may not have been the same spot. It had all the same empty qualities, as well as all the rocks. They all thought it was the perfect place as they gushed about the virtues of this nothingness. I was thinking, *If you say so*, but I was dubious. All their "look at the beautiful views" didn't help, though, in their defense, they were able to picture it after the rains, while all I saw was brown. Somaliland is very different at the end of the dry season. On this visit, I did not think Abaarso was beautiful in the least, but I desperately wanted a place for my project. We would build in Abaarso.

9

CLANS

I returned to the United States to continue organizing the school from there, and Khadar sent me pictures of a dinner that symbolized the completion of the land transfer. He informed me that it temporarily needed to be put in his name. He said he'd transfer it over to the school as soon as the school's government filings were complete.

Like Billeh, Khadar was part of the Isaaq clan, as were the vast majority of Somaliland people, probably totaling a few million and 80 percent of the Somaliland population. I thought that there was no difference from one Isaaq to another. I thought clan was only relevant when there was a conflict with another major Somali clan, such as the Darod, who border the Isaaq on the east, or the Hawiye, who live in Mogadishu, the capital of Somalia. I know all Isaaq clansmen remember the pains of their civil war, when the Somali dictator, who was not Isaaq, laid waste to their cities. It is true that on this level the Isaaq clansmen are all united, but it turns out that is only a surface-level understanding of how clans impact Somaliland society.

I approached the concept of clans from my limited knowledge of the Rwandan genocide. In Rwanda, you were either a Hutu or a Tutsi, and that was where the difference among the clansmen ended. If two people are Tutsis, then they are on the same team. I assumed the same was true for members of the Isaaq clan. But when Isaaq clansmen are dealing within their own clan, the fact that they are both Isaaq becomes irrelevant, and all that matters is their subclan. Three Isaaq might be united against a Darod, but that doesn't mean the three Isaaq view one another as equals. If two of them are from one subclan and the other from another, the two who are from the same subclan will be expected to stick together against the third. If all three are from the same subclan, then you go down another subclan layer to where they split, and once again the two who are closer family are expected to be united. And thus it continues, through sub-sub-subclans, all the way down to choosing one's brother over one's cousin.

Within the Isaaq clan, Billeh and Khadar were on different lineage tracks from the very first Isaaq split many centuries ago. I knew that Billeh's clan led back to his home in Erigavo, but I didn't know anything about Khadar's, nor did I know it would be relevant. As it turned out, Khadar traces his subclans down numerous layers until finally landing on the clan whose ancestral home is Abaarso Village. Khadar had grown up in Hargeisa, but clan-wise, Abaarso is his family's historic home and its inhabitants are his people. For better or for worse, I would build my school in his territory, though I didn't know it at the time.

Khadar's clan ties to Abaarso Village had made the land acquisition for the school easy and explained why Khadar had bypassed the vast open spaces between Hargeisa and Abaarso. From his perspective, he could easily connect with the local people and make his pitch. If any of them gave him trouble, then he could call on elders in common who could sit everyone down and make peace. At the same time, if Khadar promised the school to a different village, then his clansmen would be furious and would demand to know why he'd help another village instead of theirs. Bringing a successful school to his own village would gain him glory among his clansmen. It would also gain him a tremendous amount of control, as even the Somaliland government will rarely challenge a clansman in his home village. My school being built in that village would inextricably link the school and Khadar in the minds of all Somalilanders. Given the significance of the clan connection, I would regret not knowing about it sooner.

Next Khadar connected me to a Somali architect in Atlanta, Georgia, to draw up the plans for the multibuilding complex. The architect was also clan-connected to Abaarso Village. The architect, a man by the name of Amin, provided some early drawings free of charge. I liked Amin and felt he truly cared, and while I didn't go with all his designs, we did use his drawing for the main school building. This would include six classrooms, a larger lecture hall, a library, a staff office, and a cafeteria. It was to be the first phase of construction, and with designs in hand Khadar said he would get quotes from Somaliland construction companies.

When Khadar came back with the construction quotes, the numbers were much higher than he'd first estimated. Rather than building our school for $500,000, which he had told me was sufficient, the price for full construction was now looking to be at least $1 million. This was a major setback, but Khadar assured me that my $500,000 was more than enough for me to personally donate. He said Somalis were used to talk of projects that never happened, but once they saw our construction starting, they'd come up with wood, cement, and whatever else we needed. If I started it, then the Somali community would come up with the rest. I didn't know if I believed this, though I certainly wanted to.

At the construction site, the first thing built was a perimeter wall. Then ground was broken for the school's academic building. Khadar would periodically send me pictures, and I loved watching the progress, as well as the construction methods, which were so different from ours. Rather than using machines to dig, workers used hand tools for all the construction work. They even made the concrete blocks on-site, mixing the cement and putting it into molds. Trucks brought in dirt and rocks, as well as stacks of cement bags. When they weren't transporting materials, they were transporting workers. Dozens of laborers were now transforming the hilltop. Outside the school's new walls, a tiny economy of makeshift shops had formed to serve the workers.

Despite the promising start, work didn't progress as quickly as I had hoped. Before long I made another trip to Abaarso. I spent a couple of weeks in Somaliland working out the remaining phases and details of the project. Khadar and I discussed where to get the furniture and supplies; how to contract with purveyors for food; how to outfit the school with day-to-day supplies, water, power; and everything in between. Feeling assured that construction would continue apace, I returned home to

Boston and kicked into overdrive. With less than three months until my next trip to Somaliland, I needed to pack up my life in America, prepare our teachers for travel, and ship supplies and books. I had discovered Books for Africa, an organization whose mission is shipping books and computers in order to end the "drought of books" in Africa. It would still cost us almost $10,000 for the shipping costs, but it was worth it to fill the library in one stroke. I also had to figure out how to deal with the remaining construction delays. Then I would be moving to Somaliland to assume my role as headmaster of the Abaarso School.

10

TEACHERS

To no one's surprise, recruiting teachers would prove challenging. Folks were not all lining up to work in a not-yet-constructed, armed compound for a not-yet-started school in a breakaway region of the world's number one failed state. What I could sell was the promise of the school and Somaliland's track record for safety.

At the time, Al Shabaab, the Somali terrorist organization linked to al-Qaeda, was in control of the vast majority of southern Somalia, including the capital, Mogadishu. When I first started my recruiting effort, they had yet to make inroads in Somaliland, but a few months later they bombed three sites in Hargeisa: the presidential palace, the Ethiopian embassy, and the UNDP (United Nations Development Programme) headquarters. It was against this backdrop that I was trying to convince teachers to come to Somaliland. And yet they still came.

My first hire was Kiette, a young woman who was already working for an NGO and was interested in changing to a different organization. She was short with blond hair and, depending on her expression, could look as young as eighteen or as old as thirty-two. As it turned out, she was twenty-four, was a graduate of Northeastern University, and desperately wanted to be working "in the field." She had little interest in a typical life track and saw herself living in a place like Somaliland. Kiette quickly became the "manager" of everything, frantically running around, but smiley and always willing to take on more. She would ultimately spend a couple of years working with me, and finding crucial recruiting websites would be her first contribution of many. We also did campus recruiting, and one by one we brought a core group of five teachers into the fold. They were an eclectic bunch of varying ages, nationalities, and temperaments: Anthony, fresh out of Harvard; Vigdis, a public school teacher from California; Colin, a Canadian citizen with a BA in history and philosophy; Daniel, a citizen of Mexico with an undergraduate degree in engineering, an MS in materials science, and a PhD in physics; and Tom, the eccentric math teacher.

Tom was my favorite of the teachers who arrived the first year. A skinny twentysomething, he grew up in Minnesota and had most recently lived in Yemen. He was a math major who loved everything about the subject, from simple arithmetic to areas way over my head. Tom was also extremely handy. That was a good thing because quality local furniture was hard to come by. Tom built basic shelves and tables to fill out the school's needs.

About a month before the teachers were scheduled to arrive, Al Shabaab was once again all over the news. The terrorist group had been warning NGOs in southern Somalia that an attack was imminent. In 2008, there was so much violence against educational facilities that all of the schools in Mogadishu were temporarily closed. It wasn't long before family members of my small group of teachers were calling me to express their personal alarm. All I could do was reassure them that we were going to Somaliland, not Somalia, and Somaliland was a much more peaceful place. Thankfully, none of my teachers backed out. They were pioneers and adventurers, willing to come despite the danger and the fact that my school wasn't even open yet.

By the middle of August, all of our teachers were in-country. In addition to the teachers and Kiette, there was Keith, who used to work with me at my hedge fund and was now here looking at business opportunities; and soon Daniel's Ukrainian girlfriend, Genia, would join the staff.

The teachers' contracts committed them to one year. Staying for more than one year required extraordinary dedication because living in Somaliland wasn't easy for a Westerner. There were no bars or clubs.

There were extremely few social opportunities. The Internet in the country was very poor, making it hard to keep up with friends and family back home. Abaarso itself was an extremely isolated location, and safety precautions made it even more so. What's more, I was, of course, demanding. This was about hard work, not about travel, sightseeing, or fun.

Where I could, I tried to improve teachers' lives. The teacher housing was actually reasonably nice, an apartment with a bedroom, sitting area, and a private bathroom. Teachers had their own cook, a young Somali woman named Nimco, who we all grew to love. Once you showed her a dish, she'd be able to consistently make it better than you had. Keith taught her fajitas, which were an immediate hit. Somehow she learned to make pizza, even making her own dough. In addition to providing a cook, we also did the teachers' laundry, another service they definitely did not have back home. Still, several teachers found my attempts to improve their quality of life far from sufficient. Perhaps they were right and I should have done more, but for me staff amenities were beside the point. They'd signed up to build something special, they knew they were coming to a start-up school in a war-torn country, and the students deserved our complete focus.

11

THE ABAARSO CONDITION

With the exam finished and school about to start, tuition is a big issue for a lot of our incoming students. Now, Amal Mohamed, who wanted SOS Sheikh to the point of tears, is totally on board to come to Abaarso, but her family and the parents of two other accepted girls from her home city of Burao are asking for a "group discount." They are by no means alone in asking for financial aid. Many students are pushing for reduced tuition, and I feel obligated to grant their requests. After all, I am in no position to judge who can pay and who cannot, and in each case we are talking about such small amounts. How can we let a handful of dollars stand in the way of a kid's education?

A few days after acceptance day, I am in my office when a young incoming student named Mohamed Hussein knocks on my door. He wears what appears to be a new outfit—blue dress shirt, black dress pants, and a pair of fresh white Air Jordan sneakers, which I'm sure are knock-offs. He beams, but in a nervous kind of way. He is accompanied by his father, a large man who looks to be in his late forties, and dressed in a much more customary way, complete with a *mawiis* and a nice scarf neatly folded over one shoulder. There is a third man—Abdi Suudi from Djibouti, a family friend, who speaks English well enough to be their translator.

"This is Chief Abdirahman Hussein," Abdi Suudi says, gesturing toward Mohamed's father. "He is a tribal leader and well-respected man. His son, Mohamed, wants to accept the admissions offer, but the chief has only a small income derived from a welding shop."

The father-and-son team stand quietly beside him. Abdi adds that the chief has many children, another reason that he cannot afford to pay. He then presents me with a letter carefully written in English by a religious leader of their region, which essentially states the same thing, just another angle of support.

I take a good look at Mohamed, standing there with his dad and his dad's friend. The fact that the chief and his son have recruited Abdi to make the appeal is remarkable. Djibouti is fourteen hours away on a good day, assuming you have a way to travel between the cities. I have no idea about this kid, only that a big effort is being made. He sweats anxiously and almost prays with his eyes that I let him in.

"Mohamed can come to Abaarso for free," I say, my message instantly translated for the family by Abdi. Upon hearing the translation, Mohamed looks half elated, half full of fear, but definitely relieved.

"However, there is a condition," I continue, my comments quickly translated sentence by sentence. "I want Mohamed to make me two promises. First, he will strive to be the best student in the entire school. He should work as hard as he can to achieve this. Second, someday, when he's in my position, he'll do the same for someone else."

Mohamed stands there with stoic joy. The terms I have put on him pale to the fact that I have accepted him. He has been absolutely terrified that I am going to say no. After all, why would a headmaster from the United States who was opening a brand-new school take a chance on a Somali kid like him, especially when he can't even pay?

After the group leaves, I look up Mohamed's entrance examination. He is one of the last students we've accepted, and his scores are weak across the board, so it isn't like English is his only weak link. *Oh no*, I think, figuring I have just set this kid up for failure.

A short time after, two more boys arrive at my door. One of them is Mubarik, the formerly nomadic boy who missed the Sheikh cut and ended up at Abaarso for alphabetical reasons, and I do not recognize the other young man. Neither of them speaks English, so I find someone to translate for me. Mubarik gets right to the point. "I was accepted to Abaarso, but I can't pay the fees," he says rapidly. "I'd like my friend here to take my position."

This isn't the same kind of conversation I had with Mohamed's family. Mubarik isn't bargaining or posturing, he is defeated. I know he is one of my most qualified students, and I feel sad seeing his resignation to a lesser life. Here is a society with so little, and he's come to feel that even what is available in his poor country is unattainable due to his financial position. I'd never thought before about someone with $100 of monthly income being so much wealthier than someone with none. It is more than I can take and I can't let him get away. I tell him he is coming to Abaarso, and I give him a full ride. As with Mohamed, the condition is that he excel academically and pay it forward someday. As for his friend, I am unable to add him to the charter class. We must keep standards on who has earned his way, and this boy hasn't.

Mohamed and Mubarik have both been offered a once-in-a-lifetime chance for success, or at least that's my opinion of Abaarso. They are both beyond grateful, especially now that tuition is no longer an issue. But this crazy launch at a strange new school elicits different reactions in each boy.

Mohamed is so happy that he cries during the car ride home to Hargeisa. He no longer has to go to a public high school, his fate had he not gotten the tuition offer. In public school, he had teachers who were themselves poorly educated and yet were handling the daunting task of teaching eighty to a hundred students in one classroom. Poor performance would not impact their excellent job security, a situation all too similar to what we see in the United States. Had he continued on that track, Mohamed feels he would have reverted back to his old habits and lifestyle, not focusing on school much and playing soccer to ease his boredom.

Mohamed also wants to get away from the city and all the stresses that come with it, but mostly the soccer mob mentality. He says it's not so much the games themselves but the aggression that happens before, during, and after the matches when team members go out into the neighborhood looking for people to beat up, either members of the opposing team or its fans. This was the life Mohamed was living before his pro-education parents intervened.

Mubarik is on his own, having left his nomadic family several years earlier. He has been living off friends in Hargeisa, feeling more scared than joyful, maybe even unworthy because of his poverty. Mubarik is a constant reminder that even within a poverty-stricken community there are different levels of disadvantage. During the acceptance day welcome, when he had seen me and the other teachers speaking English, he had felt so overwhelmed and frightened that he wanted to run out of the room. He has come around, but he still feels intimidated. Like Mohamed, he wants an education more than anything. He still dreams of building trucks, like the ones he saw in the desert when he was a child.

In the coming few months, I try to meet all of the students and familiarize myself with their strengths and weaknesses. They need to know that I see them, I am here with them, and I'll be with them on their tough climb ahead. This will take a lot of work, and I find some students harder to reach than others. They will take more time. I am also up against some superficial barriers. For instance, I am struggling badly with their names, and my calling someone by the wrong one will not help them feel connected.

Particularly challenging is that so many of the boys have the same first name. One particularly common one is "Mohamed," the name of the Islamic prophet, and undoubtedly the most common name in the country, with many first sons receiving this name. In addition to Mohamed, there are boys named Mohamoud, which at first I don't realize is actually a different name. Complicating matters further is that there are also multiple derivatives of "Abdi," such as Abdikarim, Abdirahim, Abdirahman, Abdisamad, and Abdiladif. Because "Abdi" means "servant," and there are ninety-nine different names for Allah, there are ninety-nine different names that can be formed by using Abdi, plus one of the names for Allah. As an example, Abdirahman translates in Arabic to "servant to the one who is most merciful," whereas Abdikarim is "servant to the one who is most generous."

The use of Abdi is so widespread in Somaliland that you often see it listed in shorthand—A/karim for Abdikarim and A/lahi for Abdilahi.

And if that isn't enough to learn, in Somali the letter *c* is actually a guttural *a* sound, which I can't hear or make. Spelled in Somali, "Abdi" is actually "Cabdi." So now, Abdikarim, Cabdikarim, A/karim, and C/karim are all different spellings for the exact same student. And our student by that name chooses a fifth way of further shortening C/karim: he calls himself CK.

Our class has eight different boys whose first name starts with "Abdi," including one student whose name is Abdirahman Abdisalan Abdilahi. I get to know him early on, initially as "Abdi Abdi Abdi." The class also has three Ahmeds, a Mohamoud, and six Mohameds. At one point, I look at a list and see that I can identify everyone except for a boy named Mukhtar and a handful of the Mohameds. I fix this in one stroke. A teacher points out Mukhtar, and from then on, any boy I don't know I just call Mohamed.

A statistician could look at Abaarso's student body and give a bunch of metrics: 100 percent Somali students, 74 percent boys, 64 percent from Hargeisa, and so on. I'm a finance person and I love statistics, but my job is to see each student for who he is; an individual with certain abilities, insecurities, dreams, and fears. I need to know the students so that I can best motivate them while also working through the issues holding them back.

People use the word "miracle" when describing what would be needed to take these students from Somaliland to success in U.S. higher education, but I don't think a miracle is necessary. What we need is for the students to believe it is possible, so that they will give it all they have and won't stop until reaching their goal. That belief—nurtured by motivated and educated teachers—fuels tenacity and focus. It can go a long, long way.

PART THREE

SCHOOL CULTURE

*The most unprofitable item ever manufactured
is an excuse.*

—John Mason

12

MOHAMED: A DAY IN THE LIFE

The campus mosque calls out the four thirty a.m. prayer. Mohamed Hussein hears it and comes to life. A lot to do today. A lot to do every day, including five daily prayers. Mohamed sleeps in the mosque as well as prays there. He has been selected by his peers to be one of the mosque leaders, a great honor. In fact, by choice he now sleeps in a small room behind the big prayer space instead of in the dorms with the boys. Each morning, he goes down to the boys' dorms and knocks on each and every door to wake them up. The prayer lasts for ten minutes, after which most students go back to sleep. But Mohamed spends the next two hours before first period studying. He finds these two hours to be the most productive of the day. He memorizes new vocabulary, does SAT (which stood for Scholastic Aptitude Test, now Scholastic Assessment Test) math, and finishes some other homework. Almost two years in, he now knows advanced words, the kinds one finds in the books he wants to be reading. His slang and jargon are still catching up, and there are holes in some of his basic English, but they are getting filled in with practice every day.

Mohamed couldn't speak any English when he arrived at Abaarso; he didn't understand a word I said in our first meeting, and his writing skills in the language were extremely limited. Although his parents support his education, they aren't educated people. They always motivated him to excel in school, but they couldn't provide much assistance.

Mohamed's father lost his own father at the age of three. By the age of twelve, he was financially supporting his mother and younger brother. He worked at a carpentry shop until noon and then went to school until the evening. At the age of eighteen, Mohamed's father married and acquired full ownership of the carpentry shop. That year was indeed his last year of formal education, and he dropped out in the middle of his senior year of high school.

Mohamed's mother was born in a small village deep in the countryside. She grew up tending to the cattle of her nomadic family. Like many Somali nomad families, her family herded their cattle all year long. The prospect of receiving an education was at best an improbable dream. Nonetheless, his mother moved to Hargeisa in her early teens in hopes of going to school. Yet the Somali civil war soon left the country and her dream in shambles.

Mohamed's parents sacrificed to ensure that he and his seven siblings had schooling from an early age. Though they struggled financially, his father made sure the children didn't miss a day of school, paying whatever school fees he could afford. Mohamed credits his parents for instilling in him a great work ethic, a deep sense of gratitude, and an insatiable appetite for learning.

Mohamed thanks God that he has gotten into Abaarso, although here the pressure is on, especially with the all-English policy, which threatens to overwhelm him. Soon after arriving, he called his father to say it was too hard for him and he wanted to quit, but his father told him he must stick with it.

I've started hearing from teachers that Mohamed is memorizing every word for every object, that he is memorizing the words from the dictionary along with their definitions. Whenever I see him, he is either studying or memorizing words. If he goes to play soccer with the other boys, he has his flash cards with him for before and after the game. One time, I ask him about objects in the room. I give him the word "pillow," and he gives me a textbook definition. I say, "Yes, Mohamed, but you could simply have pointed to this," as I pick one up to show him. For "bed," he says "A long piece of furniture with four legs that people lie on to sleep."

On most days, Mohamed gets to breakfast a little before his seven a.m. class. The lines for breakfast are always long and the atmosphere very competitive. Breakfast is usually *laxoox*, a spongy, pancake-like bread similar to the Ethiopian *injera*. It is served on a metal plate, accompanied by a cup of tea, Somali-style, essentially overly sweet black tea with ginger, a couple of other spices, milk, and a preposterous amount of sugar. Most of the kids eat the meal with their hands, cupping the bread like a spoon; some mash up the *laxoox* and pour the tea on it first. When we had built the cafeteria, we had intended for it to be coed, but not long into the first quarter, we learned that the girls didn't like to eat where the boys can see them, so now we've set up a separate cafeteria for the girls.

After breakfast, Mohamed heads to his first class. A full day is six hours of actual class time divided into eight subjects: two different English classes, Arabic and Islamic Studies, two math classes, history, a science class, and computers. The first year, the subjects offered had been shaped by which teaching skills were available, but with time, the schedule had more or less settled down.

Most kids have a favorite class, and Mohamed's is history because it quenches his thirst to know more about the world; more important, it is the first time that he is taught Somali history. He would never have imagined that the only place he would learn Somali history is in an Abaarso classroom with a foreign teacher. The history class has instilled in him a deep sense of pride in his identity as a Somali. Moreover, it lights what will be an inextinguishable fire within him to critically scrutinize the education system that is failing to inspire Somaliland students.

The classrooms at Abaarso are good-sized, with off-white walls, tile ceilings, and whiteboards up front. The desks are the individual seats with the arm table, so every student has his or her own personal work space. Girls and boys sit on opposite sides of the room, which happened starting on the first day, without any prompting from us.

Classes end just before two p.m., at which point students eat lunch. This is now traditional siesta time in Somaliland, as the sun is too hot to do much, but you'll rarely find Mohamed resting. Around four p.m., the campus will come to life again with sports, science club, community service, and student jobs on campus. Mohamed joins a few of his classmates to play pickup soccer on a cement tennis court between two cement basketball blacktops. On the regular soccer field, he plays right back for the Abaarso team. Prior to a game, he prays the afternoon prayer in the mosque, and then he immediately goes to the field. He plays until sunset, when evening prayer time comes.

After evening prayer, he rushes to the dining hall to beat the dinner line. After dinner, he attends an all-school study hall from eight to ten p.m. in the school's spacious auditorium. Finally, he goes to bed around ten thirty p.m. to prepare himself for a very early wake-up before the morning prayer at four thirty a.m. Then it all starts over.

Mohamed is gaining at least three academic grade levels each year. And he'll need that, having started ninth grade at first-grade English and third-grade math. Far removed from the boy in my office twenty-one months earlier, Mohamed ends his tenth grade at Abaarso by getting close to a high school level. Few people would push themselves the way Mohamed has, but he shows no signs of tiring. To the contrary, he seems to be just getting warmed up. Energized by his success, he believes the sky is the limit and sees nothing that can stop him.

Mohamed is the kind of student to build the program around. We publicly reward him, praise his tenacity, and challenge others to follow in his footsteps. He leads the students by the strength of his example. Tenacity cannot be taught in a classroom, but it is a lesson that a school can promote every day.

13

STRAIGHT TALK AND MOTIVATION

Walking across the campus, I spot Qadan Mohamed, a student admitted in our second year, fifty feet away. It is time we have that talk. Qadan was born with one arm, a disability that made her a burden to her nomadic family. She was one of twelve children, but she would be unable to do the physical labor that their way of life demanded. Her family believed she would be a failure in the role of the traditional Somali woman, and she would be less desirable for marriage. When she was six years old, her mother took her to live with her aunt in Burao, more than six hours from their nomadic base on the border of Ethiopia. Her mother thought that at least in Burao, a city of over one hundred thousand, she could get an education and maybe, with an education, have a life of some sort.

Qadan, though, felt abandoned and unloved. She didn't see her mother or father again for nearly six years, and after that, only sporadically. She was appreciative that her aunt had taken her in, but this woman had older children of her own, too old for them to be companions for Qadan. With her disability and enormous sense of abandonment, she sometimes felt like she didn't fully belong, that the world would be better without her. Nonetheless, her aunt faithfully oversaw her early education, which began in Quranic school, followed by primary school.

Her score on the entrance exam was good enough to get into Abaarso, although her first choice had been SOS Sheikh, something I often playfully remind her of.

Qadan's uncle is paying her Abaarso tuition despite having more than twenty-five children of his own spread across four different mothers. He isn't rich, but he takes his responsibilities seriously, and he wants to see his niece educated. A year later, he will move his son from SOS to Abaarso and bring two daughters as well as another niece to the school. In time, he'll have a dozen of his children and nieces at Abaarso.

I have decided to deal with Qadan's handicap the same way I deal with most of the students' issues, by being caring and frank. I am sure Qadan spends a lot of time feeling self-conscious about her arm, and I've seen her trying to hide her handicap. But there's little she can't do, having gotten so good with the other arm that six months in, many of the teachers didn't even notice that one was missing. When I mentioned her disability to a teacher, her shocked response was quickly echoed by several others sitting within earshot.

"Can we talk a minute?" I ask Qadan, causing her to pause. "I hope you don't mind, but I want to ask you how you came to have one arm."

She explained that she was born this way, so it was not an injury, an illness, or an accident. She has never known life any other way.

"Well," I respond. "I've heard nothing but good things about you.

"You are making a great effort in and out of classes," I continue. "The teachers tell me you are very bright, and I know you are even playing sports with the girls. So I'm going to tell you something important and I hope you're listening."

"Okay," she replies, focusing in. By the nature of my position as headmaster, I tend to get attentive audiences. It is likely all headmasters do, which is an opportunity they should not waste.

"You are intelligent and you have a great work ethic," I tell her. "Most people would love to have those. I can only imagine that you spend time wishing you had both arms and envying people around you. You've been given important gifts, and you're headed to be so well educated. Don't waste your time thinking about what you don't have or wishing you were someone else. Many of them should be wishing they were you."

No one has ever said something like this to her before, and it sticks with her. She will still quote the conversation years later.

I can see a social worker being horrified at my bluntness, but then, they might feel that way about countless of my other direct conversations and confrontations. I talk to students like the adults I want them to be. They have enormous obstacles ahead, and they need encouragement and advice. Qadan already has the deck stacked against her, and she can't afford to add unnecessary psychological or self-pity blocks to the mix. None of the students can. Maybe my approach wouldn't work with everyone, and it is probably not the right one for kids from greater privilege. But so far it is working with Abaarso kids. Most appreciate that with me they know what is what and I don't sugarcoat any of it. They don't like an overly politically correct approach, either, and find coddling to be wishy-washy or seemingly fake.

Like most of the people I knew, I grew up knowing I had a safety net. While my father was always on the verge of bankruptcy and my mother always worried about money, I still grew up middle class. Among other things, I always knew I'd be able to access higher education. Being an American citizen does provide you with a number of safety features, such as access to federal funding for college in the form of grants and loans. Colleges also give substantial financial aid to qualified American students who can't otherwise afford it. I am not arguing whether or not there needs to be more, just pointing out that college is realistic for an American kid who achieves. An underprivileged student might feel hopeless, but it is that *feeling* that needs to change more than the reality. Higher education *is* available.

Compare that to Qadan and the other Abaarso students. They have no education safety net. The U.S. government doesn't fund foreign students to come to American colleges, and the universities in their home country are of such low quality that few graduates are employable as professional workers. I know several of the leading businessmen in Somaliland, and despite the massive unemployment of the country's youth, the businessmen have no choice but to fill their technical positions from beyond their borders. This leaves the young Somali graduates frustrated and looking for something better. In some parts of Somalia, they've joined

Al Shabaab, the Islamic terrorist organization, at least getting money and some respect. In Somaliland, the kids leave by the dozens to perform *Tahrib*, the Somali word for illegally migrating to Europe. Some will die on the horrifying and dangerous trek. Capsized boats have claimed untold numbers of lives since this migration began. Some will get no farther than Libya, where profiteers will take advantage of them, and even those who successfully cross will probably end up in refugee camps. I learned that one teenage girl who had visited the school drowned off the coast of Malta. Only a few years earlier, she had represented Somalia in the Olympics, running track and field. I haven't gone across the world to have Abaarso students suffer the same tragedies. They want more, too, and they don't want me whitewashing conversations. I have a knowledge and background that they don't, and they want me to lead them until they reach the point when they can lead themselves. Shouldn't guiding children to self-sufficiency be a major goal of education?

I have another terrific kid, a girl named Muna, who arrived at Abaarso at only twelve years old, with our average ninth grader being more like sixteen. When she plays basketball with the other girls, she gets blocked on every shot she puts up, but it doesn't stop her from trying and smiling the whole time. She is like everyone's little sister, and the whole campus adores her.

Muna was on a fantastic academic rise and well on her way to success, but then I heard from teachers that she had suddenly not been herself. She was no longer diligent, no longer focused. Her father was dying back in her home village, and that now had her mind.

The next time I saw Muna, I sat her down to relay one of the most powerful events from my teenage years. My mother had a great friend in Worcester, who had a nice husband and two good children, the older girl college-age and responsible, the teenage boy sweet but rebellious and wild. I remember seeing *Jurassic Park* together, when the boy declared out loud to the theater that it should have been called "Jurassic Fart"— he had that kind of sense of humor. He just wanted to have some fun.

Then, when he was still a teenager, he overdosed and died. For his parents, the worst nightmare had come true. Figuratively speaking, his mother pulled a blanket over her head for month after month, unable to cope. But she herself wasn't well. She had a liver disease that needed to be managed with medication. When her pills ran out, she didn't have the will to refill them. Maybe a half year later, she visited the doctor, but he told her it was now too late. Not long after, she, too, died, leaving her husband and daughter, both of whom still needed her. In her last days, she told my mother, "I never meant for this to happen." As for me, I never forgot those tragic words of regret.

I send Muna home to spend time with her father, telling her to make sure she talks to him about everything she ever wanted to. I tell her that when she returns, she needs to focus again. Every father wants to know that his child will be okay, and she should work to do him proud. When Muna comes back, she is her old self again. She has resolved her panic about never seeing her father again, and she knows there is no unfinished business. Months later she comes to me and, with her typical charm, says, "Don't worry. I am taking my medicine."

Between them, our students have been through everything imaginable and then some. One orphaned boy lived with his grandmother along with his aunts and cousins. When he is in our eleventh grade, one of these aunts goes crazy, setting herself and her two little children on fire, killing all three. How could anyone not cry for that kid? Or for the girls who have constant headaches because their older brothers have been kicking them in the head since they were little? They know I care, listening to what they have to say, sometimes not holding back my own tears. They need empathy, but they also need strength. I hope they can see that I relate to them, and that no matter how sad the past or how rough the present, together we'll work until they are at a place where they are in control, a place where they can stop other children from suffering the same tragedies. I think that's why they listen to me when I push them to strive for something better.

In their world, which has no safety net, Abaarso becomes a buoying presence that will give them back everything they put in. It isn't unconditional support; in fact, our conditions are steep. But, in time, students come to learn that if they follow the three Abaarso values—tenacity, critical thinking, and integrity—then Abaarso will always be there supporting them.

Even the very best students need extra help. Deqa is a dominant student who loves all aspects of learning, but she has her own demons she needs to face. Many have personal issues, and two of my advisees, Amal and a boy we will call Hassan, are not meeting reasonable expectations. I can't do their work for them, but I can work on their attitudes. Specifically, that everything is someone else's fault.

Amal furiously walks through the hall toward my office. "Jonathan," she barks, "I need to talk to you."

"What's going on?" I ask.

"That b—— just gave me a D." Amal's English is strong and her cursing fluent.

Hassan uses a different version of the same "fault deflection." I am meeting with him at the end of the term to go over his grades.

"Hassan, you are much better than this," I say, presenting him with his report.

"Let me explain," he answers. "A proper grade weighting system would take the following into account. . . . The history teacher is not weighting his grades properly. . . ." and on and on, one excuse after another.

I have decided tough love with both Amal and Hassan is the only way. I tell them that they've both told me the last excuses I am ever going to listen to, and I cut them off every time they try to tell me another. Succeeding at Abaarso is on them, and they need to do better.

From this I develop a mantra, which increases in intensity over the years. "The world doesn't care about your excuses. In fact, it usually doesn't give you a chance to tell them." I am not arguing whether a student's excuses are legitimate; I am not denying the pain of the student's past, and I am not saying that I don't care. The student could come to me at any time to talk, but I won't be the one evaluating his or her future college or job applications.

14

FAHIMA'S ROCKS

I walk out of the teachers' compound on a Wednesday afternoon at four thirty, the beginning of a Somaliland weekend. The sun is no longer at its peak, so hopefully with sunglasses and a hat, my pale skin won't burn. The day is so predictably warm and windy that it could be any day of any month, at least one that doesn't have rain. I, too, now have my predictable routine.

We have established a project to make pathways between our buildings, a great effort because the area is blanketed with rocks of all sizes. As usual, my work partner is already digging her *sabrat*, her iron spear, into the earth, pulling up another rock that had been tarnishing the path. She's covered up, like all the girls, but her skinny fingers show that she probably weighs only eighty pounds. I hand her a carrot, one of the few foods I know she'll eat. I don't know how a human can survive on so little food, never mind one who brings the intensity to a day that this young woman brings to each hour.

"Hmm," she says, looking up at me for a second. She says this with a huff that is hiding a smile. She's clearly glad I've arrived but is also implying that it is about time I showed up. She has brought a *sabrat* for me, too, and now the two of us are digging up rocks.

"Why do we do this?" I ask, testing her.

"Because it is worth making our world even a little better," she replies, adding, "The rocks we move don't move themselves back." My protégé has been listening.

The civil war in the late '80s and early '90s left Somaliland all but uninhabitable. Siad Barre's Somalia military regime had fighter planes taking off from Hargeisa Airport and flying missions to destroy every rooftop and every farm in the region. From what I could tell, they succeeded, the evidence still present in village ruins across the country.

With much of the population fleeing the country, many to refugee camps, survival, rather than investment or development, became the focus. The roads are so marred by potholes that driving seems like controlling the handset in a dangerous video game. Transportation is by old cars, donkey cart, or trucks. Hargeisa Airport is a relic, something you could picture in F. Scott Fitzgerald's *Tender Is the Night* when commercial travel to remote areas was new. The cities have electricity, but much of the country is dark. Huge parts of Hargeisa are not on a water line, and the water is insufficient where it is available. This leaves people trucking water from wells at far greater cost, with the weight of the heavily loaded trucks further damaging the roads. The University of Hargeisa, the largest public university in the country, didn't open until September 2000.

To Fahima, born after the civil war, habits such as littering without considering damage to the community are all she has ever known. She is the norm, as the majority of the population hasn't reached eighteen years of age yet. The aid industry isn't helping this mentality, either, with its handouts and quick-fix programs, none of which seem to provide much in the way of lasting solutions. Even if they do a great job, it isn't possible for a few dozen foreigners to rehabilitate a country left in ruins. The whole country's mentality needs to change away from mere survival. Millions have to join Fahima, deciding to invest their effort in making their world a little better.

I couldn't reach millions, but I could reach our students, and perhaps their perspectives could eventually go viral. This afternoon's effort already does more than teach only Fahima, which becomes clear within minutes.

Three boys walk by us on their way across campus. They stop at the spectacle of their headmaster and a frail girl spending their afternoon doing hard manual labor. One makes a motion for Fahima to hand him her *sabrat*. He starts working on a small boulder, the kind that isn't going to come out with just a few stabs. Even the least competitive among us doesn't like to lose to a rock, so this boy is certainly not done until it is out. Now one of his friends also wants to take his whacks, so he grabs the *sabrat* for a minute, making the first boy hungry to get back in. The third boy relieves me of my *sabrat* and now we have three boys doing this work. They are so focused on this particular boulder that they haven't noticed Fahima going in for more tools. Soon, all five of us are at work, "making our world a little bit better."

Some afternoons it could look like a chain gang: twenty students and teachers sharing *sabrats*, shovels, sledgehammers, even dirt-filled wheelbarrows to fill in the holes left by the removed stones. Soldiers, the guards on duty at the campus's gate, temporarily put down their guns and pick up a tool, not wanting to be left out of the action. Staff who live in the village, having finished their day's employment on campus, might put in fifteen minutes of hard work on the grounds before starting their walk home. This rock-clearing project isn't a punishment or even a plan, at least not by anyone other than Fahima and me. It may not have been traditional fun, but it is satisfying and it is a team effort. And the rocks you removed didn't go back. The students, teachers, soldiers, villagers, and I are working together, transforming our own campus.

Fahima got to Abaarso in the way that a lot of the students arrived, having *not* gotten into SOS. Like most of the others, she has realized her luck even in this very first year. But Fahima is an extreme child, and this fate is not one that in my view she takes lightly. For her good fortune, she seems to feel obligated to repay Abaarso by working tirelessly. We first started this rock removal when I realized that every afternoon she was voluntarily mopping the floors around the school. "Someone could come visit," she'd say, "and I need to make sure that the school looks great."

I believe Fahima feels that way, but I also think there's more to it. In time she would tell me about her childhood, the type of youth that no child should ever experience, the kind that can make you cry thinking about it. She is now in a new place, one that makes her hopeful, and maybe Fahima believes that if she shows all the love she can to Abaarso, then it will love her back.

Other teachers respond to her passion by telling her that she has to be less intense and try to have some fun. This only makes Fahima angry. To her, these teachers don't understand. Which brings us to another reason why we are outside cracking rocks in the midst of a small group. Fahima will be intense and extreme regardless, so at least I can involve her in a more public and social activity. Another clause in this implicit agreement is she would eat the food I bring her and work on some mental math problems. "It is now five thirty p.m., and we are eight hours ahead of New York. What time is it in New York?"—this kind of question.

Students and staff fixing up the campus started during the first days at Abaarso. Before the buildings went up, Abaarso was an empty hill riddled with rocks. It was treacherous to even walk around the land. The construction labor had cleared the rocks from each building's footprint, but you could sprain your ankle going between them. I probably could have hired a bulldozer to clear it all out, but the campus problem was less urgent than developing the "investment" culture, having the kids believe that their input makes a difference.

When Abaarso started, it was a microcosm of the problems throughout Somaliland's society—for example, the idea that littering is tolerable. Our students always threw their trash wherever, and I needed them to stop it. I used shame if I had to, letting the culprit know that his action damaged our whole community. Why should we come all the way across the world to help students who don't care enough about the school to take care of it? Heavy-handed? Probably. But also true, and these students need to hear it. Abaarso School isn't a handout. Again, Abaarso's love comes with conditions.

In the beginning, I made sure that every student came to an area of campus and started clearing it. Most hated it and didn't work hard. Those who put in the effort were referred to as "Jonathan's slaves." Some even hummed slave songs they'd heard in *Glory*, an American Civil War–themed film we showed on "movie night." Fahima's example of volunteering is the pinnacle, but it isn't the first. That credit goes to Tom, the excellent early math teacher, who gained a loyal following among the boys.

With Tom's guidance, Haibe and Zakariye, two other students, tied string to two stakes that they hammered into the ground, to make sure the path was straight. Other boys looked for large rocks that could line the path right under the string, as Zakariye, pencil hoisted behind his ear, was going to test the width at different points to make sure the two sides of each path run parallel. Tom had them measuring, calculating, and being precise. They felt like engineers. Character-wise Fahima, Haibe, and Zakariye are on their way, having already developed a love for seeing their world improve.

15

CRITICAL THINKING

From a very early age, I lived in my head and was always thinking. I never noticed what people were wearing or what they had. I lost things constantly and had an awful time finding them because my hand had placed them somewhere without my brain showing any interest in the matter. I couldn't think back to where I had been because my mind had not saved that information in the first place. My thoughts were solely focused on whatever idea had completely taken me over.

Starting when I was six, I obsessed mostly about sports. I watched the Redskins beat the Dolphins in Super Bowl XVII and fell in love with all the technical details of the plays. By the next year, I knew more about the game than most adults and was thrilled watching the Raiders' cornerbacks shut down the Redskins' receivers. I didn't leave the house on weekends because I wanted and needed to analyze every game. My loyal stuffed animals lent a hand by filling the various positions on the field and working through plays. After watching some early ESPN show about the Vince Lombardi Green Bay Packers, I had my "stuffies" all practice his famed "power sweep," making sure the correct offensive lineman pulled. My sister, Beth, three years my senior, still has a picture of Big Teddy's team lining up against Big Monkey's.

On weekends, when our family got together with my parents' friends and their kids, I often sat with the adults talking about sports. By the time I was eight, they were actually asking my opinion on strategic situations or calls.

When I was in junior high, my mother dragged me to a movie that would always stick with me. Normally I would have been happy to go, but this was something about "standing in a liver," and that just didn't sound fun. It turned out that it was *Stand and Deliver*, the true story of a math teacher named Jaime Escalante who goes into a poor high school in East Los Angeles, a place where the immigrant students don't take advanced classes, and together the teacher and students work all the way up to the Advanced Placement Calculus exam.

In the movie, Jaime Escalante introduces fractions using fruit slices, an illustrative method that promotes hands-on learning for critical thinking. But it was the change in the students that really impressed me. They came in without expectations for their futures, already feeling hopeless. Their lives were hard—that was beyond question. They had little money, gangs around them, and sick family members who didn't speak English well enough to access the health care system. At one point, a girl was studying late at night when her mother, who had worked all day, asked her to turn out the light. My mother, an educator herself, gasped in pain, telling the movie screen, "Then she can't study!"

At movie's end, eighteen of the students passed the AP exam. My mother was clapping so hard that she—not the movie—had my attention. Right before the credits, the film announced that thirty students passed the exam the next year, and seventy-three students passed a few years later. My mom burst into tears. So much about watching that movie with my mother impacted me—my mother's love for education; the great teacher, Jaime Escalante; and that, with a change in attitude, these students could overcome such obstacles to achieve something beautiful.

People have commented that it took a tremendous confidence, bordering on arrogance, to think that I could take students from Somaliland and get them to the point where they could compete in the world's best universities. I have Jaime Escalante to thank for showing me what could be done and how I could do it. I also have to thank my mother. Her reaction to *Stand and Deliver* was a lesson to her son that took on multiple levels, especially the value of education.

Nonetheless, I was a B student in high school, and by that I mean I *never* got an A or a C, only Bs. My high school adviser was dumbfounded how my best and worst subjects could all be the same. She didn't understand that my best and worst didn't matter; I was just trying to avoid grief at home. I spent all my energy on whatever was my latest obsession. For instance, when I was in high school, a friend of my uncle Eli started a magazine about University of Connecticut sports. It was called *Husky Blue & White.* He asked me to join him at the basketball training camps where media and coaches went to evaluate up-and-coming college players. It was several days, and at each break I'd go through all my notes and compare them to those of my uncle's friend. They were long days and late nights, but my mind was so happily at work that I didn't care at all. At the end of each evening, I could barely wait to wake up and start again. Eventually, we had a thoughtful enough analysis that a few Division I coaches actually paid for our report.

Despite my lackluster academic record, I got into Emory University anyway, probably because no other applicant in the country had sold a scouting report to NCAA coaches.

At Emory, I could select my courses, and I knew real ambition for the first time. I wasn't as boxed in, and with my courses challenging me, my performance changed completely. Now, I was an A student. In class, I'd generally ask more questions than anyone else, and I'd go see my professors at their office hours to argue theories. After class, my friends and I would engage in endless debates analyzing everything.

Classes in Somaliland, from the earliest grades through university, are generally run without any interaction between student and teacher, no chance for students to ask questions, no time when teachers solicit ideas or thoughts. Nothing is done to encourage critical thinking—the skill I'd learned as a child. The first time I sat in on a class in a Somaliland school, I was shocked. For the first fifteen minutes, the classroom was completely silent other than for the sound of chalk on the board as the teacher wrote down notes. This was followed by another fifteen-minute period when the students copied what was on the board into their notebooks. Periodically, the teacher would erase one set of notes and write some more, concluding the lesson by reading what was on the board aloud. Generally, these classes had sixty or more students squeezed onto wooden benches, with boys on one side and girls on the other. Other than the chalk or students acting up, they were eerily silent. When I later talked to our students, I realized that what I had seen was standard.

There was so much academic content to cover, but, with our students' background, endowing these children with critical thinking had to take priority. We would build it into the way the whole school was run, including giving a "Critical Thinking Award" each term, and it was my primary academic focus from the start. I would begin by teaching logic the very first term of the very first year.

The logic class is my chance to get my hands dirty by actually teaching. To a small extent I am improvising a logic course I had taken at Emory, but mostly I use the way I learned to think as a kid. I have no content goals, as nothing the kids will be learning to do is in itself important, just as a crossword puzzle challenges your brain but there's no value in remembering the puzzle from last Saturday's paper. All that matters is getting our students thinking.

To begin with, I show the students the rules to tic-tac-toe. Sure, our second-highest scorer on the entrance exam managed to lose in three moves. He was never able to transition from rote memorization to critical thinking, and sadly he dropped out of school after only a few months. But putting him aside, the students quickly figure out how to play each other to a draw. They make mistakes, as would kids anywhere, but they pick up the strategy quickly, moving in response to their opponents' moves.

Every couple of weeks, I introduce a different type of challenge, with the students particularly liking ones we call "dragon problems." I got these from a book called *Tricky Logic Puzzles*, and the premise is that all dragons are either red or gray and either rational or predators. Red Rational and Gray Predator dragons always tell the truth, and Red Predator and Gray Rational always lie. If you are a knight, you only want to kill the predator dragons so you must make this distinction. You walk up to some number of dragons and they start talking to you. You have to figure out what they are, based on their statements. What's more, you are color-blind, so to you, all dragons look gray.

The simplest of these puzzles would be a dragon who says, "I am a Gray Rational." From there, you can deduce that the dragon is *not* a Gray

Rational because a Gray Rational always lies, so it never says the truth that he is a "Gray Rational." Further, it can't be a Red Rational or a Gray Predator, because those dragons always tell the truth, and for them this would be a lie. The dragon is therefore a Red Predator, because that's the only one who would lie and say he is a Gray Rational. The knight should slay the predator.

When I first wrote this problem on the board, explaining the different type of dragons, I had a room full of students looking shocked. They were waiting for me to tell them how to solve it. And how tempting that was. I'd keep reminding myself to "do less, do less," because the goal was for them to be thinking. We didn't actually need to slay any of these dragons.

It only took a few days for the whole room to be busy, with students intensely working at their desks and then forming a small line to show me their answers. I'd look, point out a mistake, and send them back. Or, I'd say, "Nice work," and give them the next puzzle. They were all engaged, their brains turning, each working at his or her own pace.

Mubarik loves my logic class, and he is a natural. His struggles with English linger, but he has come a long way. In the beginning, when somebody would ask him his name, he didn't understand what they wanted to know. On his first quiz, he didn't realize he was being tested until the following day.

In my logic class, he sees that he can construct a solution without prior instruction, which is intellectually fulfilling. He solves one so easily that at first I assume he has already seen it. The problem before him goes like this: You have a faucet and a drain and two jugs, one that holds five liters and another that holds three liters. You want to measure exactly two liters and there are no markings on the jugs.

I illustrate it on the whiteboard, though my handwriting is often so bad that the students can't read it. Mubarik comes up and, with gestures and diagrams, solves the problem. His answer is to fill up the five-liter jug, then pour from the five-liter jug into the three-liter jug until the three-liter jug is full. What is left in the five-liter jug is exactly two liters.

One girl in my logic class is even better than Mubarik. A teacher is not supposed to have favorites, and of course a better one wouldn't have, but how can I not appreciate this tall, narrow-faced girl who is solving every puzzle in half the time of anyone else? She is Nimo Ismail. Her English is better than that of most of the other kids, which is certainly an advantage, but she is also extremely clever and can block out all other distractions when she is focusing on my logic problems.

Nimo is one of the rare students who had chosen Abaarso over SOS on the entrance exam, and she had scored high enough to get into SOS. As I already thought the world of her, I was surprised to learn that she was one of the walk-ins, not having scored well enough on the national exam to qualify for the SOS test. Of course, that was also a test of dishonesty, and I believed Nimo when she admitted to giving answers to others but not actually taking them herself. As more data came in, it appeared that the national exam was a very inconsistent predictor of student quality.

Nimo reported to the testing site on the day of the exam, hoping for the chance of being allowed entry as a walk-in. Indeed, luck went her way. A number of the high-scoring girls hadn't shown up, and the empty seats meant Nimo had her invitation. Many families in this conservative Muslim country would not send a girl to a boarding school, an unfortunate change from before the war when it was more common. While Nimo had come to the test that day intending to try for admission to SOS, she ended up circling "Abaarso" as her school of choice. It turned out that my presentation to the test takers that day had swayed her, in part because she liked the idea of being taught by native English speakers and in part because we were offering unique classes like computers and robotics. Mostly, though, Nimo is a contrarian thinker not shackled by what everyone else does. She trusts her judgment, and she's not afraid to take a chance. That's one reason she could dive into my puzzles while others hold back, fearing the unknown.

Nimo is the oldest of her parents' five children. She spent the first twelve years of her life in Saudi Arabia, where for a couple years her father had her studying with a Kenyan-born English tutor. Both of her parents completed high school, and her father had some college education. At age twelve, she and her siblings returned to Somaliland with their mother. The return was triggered by two things: Nimo's allergies, which might improve with a change of environment, and the fact that non-Arab people could not attend public high school in Saudi Arabia. The following year,

Nimo's father joined the family, but after a months-long job search with no prospects, he took a position in Switzerland, sending his earnings home to support his family, like so many other fathers.

From what I can see, he would much rather be with them. While Nimo rarely gets to see him, he calls her often, perhaps even daily, and she lights up every time. Unlike some of our girls, she never has to wonder if he has moved on or if he still loves her. He even calls me, using the English he knows, to find out how she is doing. Nimo's motivation for a good education is that she will be able to reunite the family once she is educated and can find a good job. I want that, too. I hope her whole family will be together when Nimo becomes attorney general or chief justice of Somaliland. I honestly believe she is capable of this future.

In my class, Nimo is a standout in every way, though I learn that she doesn't put such effort into her other classes, perhaps another reason why she wasn't a top scorer on the national exam. In fact, when she isn't interested in a subject, she races to finish the exam, so that she can read a book the rest of the period. Nimo, I realize, is just like me when I was her age, only putting effort into what interests her. She saves her energy for things she likes.

When I introduce Nimo and the rest of the kids to board games, they are an immediate hit. I like the ones that use logic more than luck and require you to react to the actions of others. Most students have never seen a board game before, so playing them is a learning experience in both strategy and social engagement. The boys are particularly drawn to Risk: The Game of Global Domination. They are quick learners and are soon adjusting their moves in reaction to those at their approach. While at first I can easily win, I will eventually need to work hard, though I can always take advantage of their Achilles' heel, an irrational desire to control East Africa.

The girls are more in favor of Clue, which is a bit more social. Each player sticks to the same character color. I am always Mr. Green, green being my favorite color; Amal, the girl I had promised that coming to Abaarso would be the luckiest mistake of her life, is always Mrs. White; Nimo, logic star, is Scarlet; and Deqa, perhaps the top student in the school, is Mrs. Peacock. The other positions rotate through a combination of girls, with Suleikha or Siham often playing Colonel Mustard, and Barwaqo taking on Professor Plum. For Nimo and Deqa, the character choices fit, as Nimo is the cunning Scarlet type, and shy Deqa is the perfect fit for the classy old Lady Peacock. Suleikha could certainly be militant, so why not the Colonel? And Barwaqo, who is affectionately nicknamed "Waqo" (wacko), is the crazy professor. By default, Amal is Mrs. White, the servant. Mrs. White is described with the adjectives "jealous" and "frustrated," both of which we teased her about at the time.

The board games not only teach critical thinking, they help the kids develop confidence. This applies across genders, although the boys need it less because they've always had sports in their lives. For the girls, these games are some of their first experiences in competition, winning, losing, strategic play, and learning to trust themselves. It is amazing how quickly their confidence blossoms. Once, I was in the Conservatory, one of Clue's nine "locations." I rolled the dice to get out, at which point Siham, a clever player herself, looked up and said, "Why did you roll? Why didn't you take the secret passageway to the Lounge?" Without a pause she answered her own question: "You must have the Lounge." At which point she picked up her pen to check that off on her sheet. She was right. I was looking for the murder room, and I had the Lounge. She had learned critical thinking without realizing it.

16

FUNDAMENTALS

Everyone knows that you don't build a house on a weak foundation, you don't have a five-year-old practice shooting on a ten-foot basketball hoop, and you don't learn to drive in Manhattan. The same "crawl before you walk before you run" approach pretty much applies to everything.

This includes education. If a student reading at a fourth-grade level is handed *The Great Gatsby*, she will get next to nothing out of it. Slogging through paragraph after paragraph of indecipherable prose could also result in her hating to read. On the flip side, a student reading at an eleventh-grade level doesn't want to read a second-grade-level book. Teaching the right level, making sure students are challenged but not drowned, is obvious and by no means brilliant. You can't go from fractions to calculus in a year, not if you actually want to understand it. As writer Jerry Jesness pointed out in his article "Stand and Deliver Revisited," which appeared in the July 2002 edition of *Reason* magazine, the Hollywood treatment of education in *Stand and Deliver* painted an overly optimistic portrait of what's possible in a short amount of time. In reality, Jaime Escalante needed a system in place over several years to establish fundamentals, and only then would he build calculus on top of them. It took him a decade to make this happen. The shiny finish didn't come until well after the foundation was solid.

When I moved to Abaarso, I had no idea what it meant to live in a war-torn country, to be recovering from the complete collapse of all systems and all institutions. When our students got to campus, even the very best were like partially built homes for which there had been no architect. The foundations were almost nonexistent, yet there were a couple of doors and windows precariously hanging in place. The house had a few stories, but the second floor couldn't bear any weight. One of our greatest challenges the first few years was figuring out what was and what wasn't sturdy. Eventually, we'd conclude that none of it was; the house needed rebuilding from the base.

In the third year, some of our top students are taking the SSAT—Secondary School Admission Test—an exam that many American boarding schools use to judge applicants. The students have been practicing with a math teacher but found out that calculators weren't allowed on the test. I heard they were panicking, so I went to talk to them.

"Look," I tell them, "you don't even need a calculator for this stuff. Any arithmetic can easily be done in your head. Let's do #4 in the practice book. That'll show you."

I open up to a geometry problem. A circle is inscribed in a square, meaning that the edge of the circle hits all four sides of the square, with the circle completely inside the square. There are four areas of the square that the circle does not also enclose. These are shaded. The problem asks to calculate the shaded areas. You are told that the circle has a radius of 1.

The SSAT exam board no doubt viewed this as a good test of how students can apply geometry. As geometry does not require a lot of foundation before high school, our students are pretty good at it. They quickly get to the heart of the problem. The shaded areas that are inside the square but not in the circle will equal the area of the square minus the area of the circle. They know a circle's area is Pi times the radius squared, so they square 1, which is still 1, and multiply it by 3.14. The answer is 3.14. They then do the next step, which is to see that 2 radii equal a side of the square. That means the square has sides that are 2, which means that the area of the square is 4.

For many who have not done geometry in some time, that last paragraph may sound dizzying. You may even have skipped it when you saw that math was involved. Don't feel bad. Solving this SSAT problem takes a reasonable understanding of geometry, and our students have that. We've done a nice job building the geometry floor of the house. That's when I see the foundation below it collapse.

"So which answer is it, *a*, *b*, *c*, or *d*?" I ask. I am able to eyeball it in a second.

"I don't know. How am I supposed to do that without a calculator?" one of our top students responds.

"What do you mean? It is 4 minus 3.14. The answer is clear."

It takes them twenty seconds to hand calculate that answer, one that should be automatic, and students taking exams like the SSAT are so pressed for time that losing twenty seconds means not getting to a later problem. Their mental math skills and understanding of number bonds, such as that 14 will need a 6 to get to 20, which will need 80 to get to 100, are nonexistent. This is a major issue, but even this isn't the real problem.

"It is .86. But the answers are in fractions."

This is true. The SSAT has given the answer choices in fractions, so the .86 needs to be converted. However, the SSAT has basically done it for you assuming you have any understanding of what a fraction is. The four choices are ⅙, $\frac{6}{7}$, and then two more choices that are both greater than 1. You don't need to calculate anything. The answer has to be $\frac{6}{7}$. This is my whole point. No calculators are needed or even helpful in the problem.

They can't answer it. Instead they start one by one converting the answer choices from fractions to decimals using long division with lengthy hand calculations. They can't rule out any, not ⅙ because it is clearly less than .50, or the two fractions that are clearly greater than 1. On the actual exam, taking three minutes on this problem would be testing suicide. Their scores would be crushed by how few problems they'd get to, and the worst part about that is that it isn't the SSAT or some "test bias" that's to blame. The test had picked up a legitimate gaping hole in our students' fundamentals.

After this session, I try the problem on Deqa, who hadn't been there. She is arguably the top student in the school. Deqa is no better at solving it. Like the others, she cannot see how a fraction relates to a decimal other than by calculating, which means she cannot *see* it at all. This further means that she won't be able to catch any mistake in calculating. What's worse, without such understanding, none of the students can actually apply math. They are just going through mechanical operations and don't know when to use them or why. The pretty geometry level has been built without any beams to support it.

Fractions are an offshoot of division, which is to say that $6/7$ is six units divided seven ways. Might they not even understand division?

"Deqa," I say, "if we have 90 kilos of rice and we use 12 kilos a day, how many days can we eat rice before we need to get more?" I know she can get 90 divided by 12, but this problem checks that she knows what division is and can apply it. She doesn't.

Digging through our library, I find fourth-grade math textbooks. One has an assessment in the back, which I have every student take. The ninth graders have now been at Abaarso for half a year. They score 50 percent. The tenth graders are at 66 percent and the eleventh graders, 75 percent. On a fourth-grade test, I'll call that a disaster.

From then on the "Orange Book" becomes famous at Abaarso. It is a Macmillan/McGraw-Hill fourth-grade textbook with an orange cover. Every student goes through it, even those already in advanced grades. You can't understand fractions without understanding division; you can't understand division without multiplication, and multiplication is just a series of additions. So future students will start by visualizing and applying addition.

This lesson in starting at the foundation, one that Jaime Escalante understood and practiced, holds true across all subjects. Yes, you can learn some chemistry before you understand basic science and critical thinking, but you won't learn it right. And, like the fourth-grade reader picking up *Gatsby*, it will be a frustrating and off-putting experience.

Let's skip ahead to a beginner English class at Abaarso, when we had a much better understanding of what we were doing. The book of choice? *Green Eggs and Ham* by Dr. Seuss. For those who don't remember, Sam is asking the other character if he likes green eggs and ham. The other character says no, but Sam won't give up. Instead, he keeps asking him if he'd like them if they were this or that, giving slight variations. *"Would you like them in a house? Would you like them with a mouse?"* Invariably, the character says no. *"I do not like them in a house. I do not like them with a mouse. I do not like them here or there. I do not like them anywhere."* This goes on and on. Nine times Sam tries, and nine times he is rejected.

Our teacher Natalie is patiently working with the class, challenging them to really think about the book in a way you would with something far more advanced. She's asking them who the characters are and what the conflict is, and she even has them predict what will happen next. The students are new to Abaarso and have never been asked to read a story this way. It is understandably challenging, as is the English, which is why Natalie is starting with a simple story using simple words.

"So what do you think will happen next?" she asks, Sam having been rejected several times already, plenty of book left to be read, and Sam now asking, "Would you eat them in a box? Would you eat them with a fox?"

Much of the room is sure of their answer. "This time he will try them," they say.

Natalie, hiding her perplexity, patiently asks them to explain why. They come up with a few explanations, but the truth is that this, too, is a very new question for them. It will take lessons like these for them to hone such a skill.

Then she turns the page.

Not in a box.
Not with a fox . . .
I would not eat green eggs and ham.
I do not like them, Sam-I-am.

Shock and disappointment fill the classroom. The start of some understanding, too.

17

INTEGRITY

It is the second half of the third year in Abaarso, and Harry, my assistant headmaster, and I have already been through hell. There has been trouble from the outside, my life threatened, hideous accusations, the school's future put at risk, and Harry almost jailed, but none of that is currently on our minds. Instead we are now forty-eight hours into uncovering a massive cheating scandal in our original class of students.

We have been interviewing student after student, slowly getting the story, occasionally getting big breaks, and calling back students to tell them we now know they were holding back. We have learned that over the last couple of years there have been several occasions when boys had broken into the staff office and stolen exams. The exams had then been passed through the grade, to boys and to girls. Seemingly every eleventh grader has been involved, even my advisees and most trusted students.

Fahima, just a ninth grader, had begged Nimo not to go see me. "It'll be too much for Jonathan," she had pleaded. "It will break his heart." But Nimo comes to me anyway, saying she wants to talk to me. We sit down on opposite sides of the cafeteria table. She is ready to tell me something, but before words come out she puts her face in her hands and cries.

Before this scandal I wouldn't have dreamed that some of our oldest students would cheat, especially when they knew more than anyone that integrity was the fundamental building block of the school. Some of the teachers would be upset about it for months, with Harry taking it the hardest. He could deal with the outside attacks because then he was fighting for our students' futures and for what was right. Now, we both wonder how these same students could do this to us. It feels personal, like being stabbed in the back.

I had seen cheating in middle school, I had seen it in college at Emory University; I had seen it on the SOS/Abaarso entrance exam, and I'd even suspended my share of students for the offense in the three years we had been operating. But these students are in their third year; they should know better. That they'd gone from cheating all the time to cheating only on occasion was not good enough.

Emory, like many colleges, had core requirements you needed to fulfill for graduation. The requirements came in different categories, one of which consisted of cultural classes, including music. I was an upperclassman when I finally stopped stalling and accepted that I needed to fulfill this requirement. History of Jazz was considered the best class at Emory, but I was unable to get a place in it. Instead I was taking History of Folk Music, and "Hey, folk can be cool, too," or so I thought. I arrived to a big lecture hall, one of the bigger ones on campus, where approximately two hundred students waited for class to begin.

The professor was a shell of a man. According to rumors, he used to be a good teacher, but his wife had left him at some point and he started drinking, or perhaps the order of that was in reverse. On a personal level, I liked him. But he was depressed and defeated, and the class was awful. The majority of the syllabus didn't even cover what any of us considered folk music.

Come the midterm exam, students didn't know what he'd test us on. Had we really learned anything? Emory was full of ambitious premeds and pre-laws. Everyone, including me, was rightfully pissed off about taking this useless class and now taking its midterm, which we all viewed as a clear waste of our time.

I don't know how many people entered that exam planning to cheat, but you needed to be blind not to see that you could get away with anything. A few students went up to the front with questions, essentially shielding the rest of the room, not that they needed the cover. There was a buzz as people talked, opened their notebooks, and even stood up and moved around. It probably started with a few students, but soon it had become a complete free-for-all. I don't believe the professor could have been that clueless, but he didn't stand a chance. He was too weak of spirit to even protest.

I didn't cheat. Cheating on exams, no matter how stupid the class, wasn't how I did things, but I did take advantage of the situation. Toward the end of the term I went to the professor's office, told him that I was one of only a handful of students who legitimately got my grade, and said I had other classes that needed my focus and didn't want to have to take his final. He agreed without the slightest resistance.

It is easy to condemn the Emory students in that classroom. They weren't children, they were high achievers, and they were representing a place with a real reputation. They were absolutely wrong in what they did. But there are also lessons to be learned. After all, Emory students do not cheat *all the time*. This was the only occasion of cheating I saw in my four years. This wasn't a bad group of students. They cheated in this class because of the surrounding factors.

The Emory students saw the class they were taking as completely useless to their lives. What's more, they were only there because of rules compelling them to be, and they knew bad luck had cost them enrolling in a really great class. They were upset, and with reason, and most important, they saw no threat of getting caught. The only consequence would be to their conscience, and some could justify that by saying the class had been inadequately taught—which is true. That explains the first handful. Then, the others see the first group cheating. They see that others are going to get an unfair edge. That could certainly make a more honest student mad. "Well, if they're going to cheat, then I guess I should get what's mine, too. I was supposed to be in History of Jazz anyway." The next thing you know, cheating on the test is almost the cool thing to do, and the followers among them pile on.

Prior to Nimo sitting before me and confirming that she has cheated, too, I even verbalized to some of the teachers that if she was involved, then I would want to hang myself. I didn't mean it, but that's how much her integrity meant to me. But, in the event, I recover quickly. My depression lasts about twenty-four hours, and then I am fine. My recovery rests on a thought that keeps running through my head: *Who told me it was going to be easy?* I had come to a place that was broken, and I couldn't be upset when I found some cracks run deeper.

The students came from an educational system that for years had condoned cheating. I'd witnessed it at the entrance exam, the first time I had seen the kids who were now my students. Later, I'd dig into the situation more, asking our students about it. They said almost everyone cheated on the national exams, and they weren't exaggerating. They meant "everyone." Education was a business in Somaliland, with tens of thousands of students attending for-profit private schools. Those schools wanted top scorers, so they could market the quality of their schools and recruit more students. To that end, most of them encouraged cheating. Some students would tell me about cheat signals they'd been taught by their teachers. From others, I heard that exam proctors would put their mobile money transfer number on the board and turn a blind eye in exchange for each student's payment. A top student was told that he was to help other students as soon as he finished his exam. One year, a national exam needed to be postponed as it was for sale in the marketplace weeks before it was to be given.

Somaliland's rampant cheating problem was just a macro version of what I'd witnessed in History of Folk Music. From what I gathered, the culture of cheating hadn't been going on for long, maybe only a few years, but when it took off, it became completely out of control. By the time I saw it, everyone knew the score, but the momentum was far stronger than the political will to stop it. I heard rumors of a school disallowing their students to cheat one year, and the parents responded so furiously that the policy was reversed. With every other school cheating in the country, why shouldn't their students cheat, too? Otherwise, it wouldn't be fair. They were just like the students in History of Folk Music who hadn't planned to cheat, but if everyone else was . . . Those who could do something about it in Somaliland were, at best, like the teacher, overmatched and overwhelmed; or, at worst, also profiting from it. That exam didn't walk itself to the marketplace.

This was the background from which students entered Abaarso. They weren't bad kids, nor could you even judge them in the same way as you could judge the Emory students. The Abaarso students were younger and far less educated; they had not been taught another way. Taking that into consideration, I allowed the three boys whose exams I had dotted for cheating to sit for a retest. After the entrance exam, we still wanted to add a dozen or so students, so we made our own test and offered it on a couple of dates, hoping to recruit the rest of the class from untapped talent. As I'd realized that cheating was part of an endemic problem, there was no reason we shouldn't let those kids learn from their mistake. Academically, one of these boys was quite strong, one was midrange, and the other was mediocre, but all three made it in.

At Abaarso, we made it clear from day one that cheating was not acceptable. The punishment was well laid out. A first offense would result in a two-week suspension. A second offense would be suspension through the rest of the year. It didn't matter if you gave answers or received them; the rule applied both ways. I guess the students thought we were bluffing, or else, cheating was so ingrained that they just couldn't stop.

The boy who had been the most egregious on the entrance exam didn't even take answers, but he couldn't stop giving them away. He became the strongest academic boy in the school, and he didn't need anybody's help, but everybody sitting next to him wanted to tap into his answers. One time, he was clearly busted and was punished along with his answer takers. Upon learning that he had been suspended for two weeks, his mother called me to say our response was wrong. She spoke enough English for our conversation. "We never punish students for cheating in Burao," she said. It was like the commercial where someone sees a friend's Head and Shoulders shampoo and says, "But you don't have dandruff."

"Don't you think that might be the problem?" I responded.

Despite our rule, the problem remained so pervasive that we moved the lunch period to the end of the day so that the students who took the exam before lunch couldn't share the answers with those who took it after lunch.

By the second half of that first year, we seemed to have the issue under control, until we caught another student cheating. Two essays were almost identical word for word. As the papers had been written by students of different genders, we knew they couldn't have worked together, so it had to be assumed that one of them had picked out the other's paper from the teacher's inbox, copied it, and put them both back. We brought the two students before a disciplinary panel to give us an oral recap of their paper. The panel now included students. In this case, Nimo was the student proctor. Clearly, the boy knew the material and the girl didn't. It isn't easy for a student to go against her peer, and I wanted Nimo to get a lesson out of this, too. At the end, I asked her opinion. She looked in pain while saying, "She couldn't possibly have written that essay." This was the girl's second offense, so she was going to be expelled.

Now, with the new cheating scandal before us, Nimo is one of the culprits. Harry and I eventually piece it all together, and we are pretty sure that we've hit on the truth. The scandal started with a weak student breaking into the staff office to steal the exam, and then giving it to one of the most popular boys. What is fascinating is not the bold behavior but rather that the exam thief never bothered to look at it himself. He broke into the office and stole an exam, which are two huge disciplinary violations, and he didn't even do it to improve his grade. He stole it to gain the approval of the cool kids, proving that some things are the same no matter where you go.

Like the cheating during History of Folk Music, the scandal started small with a few students. Others then joined in, some because they are followers, some wanting to be accepted, some feeling it is unfair if others benefit from cheating and they don't, and some for their own quirky reasons. In Nimo's case, I genuinely believe she hated that other girls were saying, "You better not tell Jonathan." Even though she is a strong person and a noble person, she is also a teenager. In her prior school, she had few friends and barely spoke. Now, she had friends and didn't want to risk losing them. I could live with Nimo still being a teenager. I could live with the followers. I could live with all of it so long as the students saw what they did, really thought about why they were wrong, and learned their lesson. Integrity, like all lessons, would need practice. No one told me we were going to be handed finished products.

In fact, looking below the surface of the third-year cheating scandal, we found some silver linings. Most of the revelations concerned events that happened well in the past, and this was for a reason. Having partici-pated a couple of times, many of the students, including Nimo, had already left the group of cheaters months before we discovered the scandal. Yes, they had participated, but they didn't need a punishment or outside shame to knock it off. These students had already been stopped by their conscience, which shows me that they learned their lesson long before I was on the other side of the table questioning them, which is another reason that I recover so fast. My kids are growing up.

18

SUZANNE'S ORPHANAGE

Suzanne, a twenty-three-year-old graduate of George Washington University, extends her right arm and catches a twelve-year-old who suddenly dashed away. Her left arm is already holding on to another boy who bolted ten seconds before. Calmly, she walks them back to their seats on a nearby stoop. They are joined by three of their friends as Nimo thanks Suzanne for her help. All five of Nimo's students return to the math problems she wrote on her movable whiteboard.

There are five such stations set up, each manned by an Abaarso student. But it is Suzanne who is in charge. She brought the Abaarso kids to the Hargeisa Orphanage today, as she does two other days each week. She is the one who keeps order, and while the orphans appreciate the student teachers, too, she's the one they truly love. One of them knows Suzanne likes turtles, so he catches them for her, and eventually she has a collection. I see these children periodically and they always proudly brag, "Suzanne is my teacher!"

Abaarso had launched a community service/outreach program with the state-run orphanage in Hargeisa. The idea was to create a win-win situation—the children in the orphanage would get extra class time, and our students would feel empowered to create positive change. All students were required to perform four hours of community service each week, which helps them value the importance of giving back to others, but equally, prepares them for their future mission of caring for and building their community once they have completed their education. After a couple of years at Abaarso, our students are showing how much they have to offer their countrymen.

Suzanne is an English teacher at Abaarso, and she also serves as a college counselor to our students, so her plate is full. Still, three afternoons a week, she and a team of Abaarso students make the drive to the Hargeisa Orphanage. Nimo is just one of the students today, and her presence isn't a surprise since she does three times the required community service. Her classmates are running similar stations in other spots in the orphanage courtyard. Suzanne and the kids have finished a day of Abaarso classes that started at seven a.m. Their last class ends at two p.m., they wolf down a quick lunch, and Suzanne gets them on the road by two thirty. With the drive time and setup, they won't get back until after six.

The orphanage tutoring hasn't always run this smoothly, not that any outsider who witnessed it would call this controlled chaos "smooth." Abaarso students tutored here for a year prior to Suzanne's arrival, but the program had been more disorganized and therefore not fulfilling for anyone. Programs don't just work; they need serious management. Not that the program's first director or the volunteer tutors were at fault. I hadn't dedicated enough supervisory manpower, so after my Abaarso kids were dropped off at the orphanage, they were left to fend for themselves. They were completely overwhelmed. The orphans lacked discipline, so getting them to focus was no easy task, made all the more difficult because we were on their turf. With little leadership and little to show for their efforts, our students dreaded going. I feared the whole "orphanage tutoring" initiative might have been a mistake and considered shutting it down.

My pessimism about the program had deep roots. I had visited the Hargeisa Orphanage on my very first trip to Somaliland, back when I was touring the country. I had been surprised that the orphanage seemed to have only a couple hundred children, an incredibly small number for the primary orphanage in a war-ravaged city of three-quarters of a million people. At the time of my visit, I hadn't realized that most of the country's orphans had been taken in by relatives. Because of Somaliland's strong clan system, Somalis take care of their own. So, when Somalis take care of their family, the term "family" casts a far wider net than it does in America. Somalis might bring home an orphaned child whose familial relation they couldn't even explain beyond being in the same subclan. It is a great credit to the society that so few orphans were in this orphanage, but there was another side to that coin. The Somali children in this orphanage had absolutely no one. They were truly alone.

It was immediately clear that the orphanage lacked a loving touch, whether or not there were so-called caretakers. The rooms were barren, with no sheets on bare mattresses, and the children were filthy. At the time of my visit, I didn't want to be judgmental. The Somali who took me saw no such need to hold back. "These kids smell," she said. "Look at the bugs around them. Their clothes haven't been washed in ages." I can still picture one little girl, probably no older than three, whose clothes were sticking to her from being damp and soiled. When I visited the nursery, the smell was so putrid that I was physically repelled from the space. *When was the last time those diapers were changed? Were there diapers at all?*

A later visit contributed to my pessimism. My mother was visiting the country. I brought her to the orphanage to see the program at work. But the male worker at the gate didn't even want to let us in. As we were talking and negotiating, a few of the little ones came over to see what was going on, at which point this worker took out a metal rod and hit them with it. These were little kids, and he was willing to strike them, even with my mother and me watching.

When Suzanne took over the orphanage tutoring she first had to convince me not to end the program. From what I had seen, our students hated going and it showed in their lack of commitment. I wondered if it was even possible to succeed in such a place. It isn't easy to provide the only hours of sanity in the course of these children's week. Just calming them enough to start the lesson was an almost impossible task.

All this made Suzanne's success at the orphanage a complete miracle. The orphans were learning and wanted to come to the program each day. She begged me to let four of them take our entrance exam, and

I agreed. When the scoring finished, her impact was clear. Suzanne's kids were the best math students in the country.

Suzanne's success came from getting our students to buy in. They needed to see what was possible, and Suzanne showed them. Her tenacity and patience were infectious, and the kids from the orphanage now dutifully followed her lead. Once committed, our students saw the change in these kids, both in their education and their happiness. As with any good teachers, they now took pride in their students' achievement. It was their students who did great on the exam, their students being accepted to Abaarso. Our student teachers beamed with pride.

As a school community service program, something I'd thought was hopeless became a model of success. All sides have benefited, and with the orphans eventually enrolled at Abaarso, the fruits were constantly on display for everyone to see. While our students themselves came from humble circumstances, there was no denying that the plight of these orphanage kids was worse. Now these kids had hope for a bright future. It was a lesson in tenacity and compassion.

At the end of that year, Mubarik gave a speech to the students. "Orphanage tutoring used to be work. Everyone hated it," he said. "Now I can see that it is the most respected activity anyone can do at Abaarso."

That was the truth. To steal another phrase from Mubarik, the orphanage tutoring became a success "because somebody loved it." Suzanne gave her heart to the place and the students followed. She had built a sustainable program in Somaliland that others would build upon in the years to come.

At the end of Suzanne's last year, we hold a special "Fun Day" at Abaarso in which all the students are split into four teams. A teacher, one who would soon be leaving Abaarso, leads each group; Suzanne is among them. The teams compete against one another in a variety of competitions all over the campus. There are sports, public speaking matches, intellectual competitions, and board games . . . even Clue! The day ends with an "Apache Relay" in which the different teams need to make three-pointers, dig up large rocks, spell tough words, and go through a whole set of other tasks including eating half a watermelon with no hands. Amal rapidly performs this and then proceeds to throw up. The students are so excited that they don't notice Suzanne constantly running back to her room, checking her messages. Her brother has been sick his whole life and now is critically ill.

I am refereeing a basketball game and Suzanne is on the court beyond me with girls from her team. I see Haibe, one of the Abaarso boys who tutors in the orphanage, running full speed from "Capture the Flag" on the opposite side of campus. He is heading straight for the court where Suzanne and her girls are playing and doesn't even notice that he's cut right through the basketball game. Normally, I'd be upset with a student for this kind of disrespect, but this time is different. In his full dash, Haibe keeps screaming out, "WE WON IT FOR YOU, SUZIE! WE WON IT FOR YOU!" It is one of the most beautiful sights I've ever witnessed. Suzanne has left her mark on the orphanage, and all those Abaarso students whose lives she touched. She'd showed so many people what it meant to truly care. It is all the more heartbreaking when later that day we learn that her brother has died.

19

SELECTION DAY

It is nearing the end of our second year, and you can feel the excitement in the air. Students, teachers, family members, and important members of the Somali community are gathered at the campus for an Abaarso open house, and the buzz is palpable. The students are on display, with science projects and math competitions for all to see, but really all anyone wants to know is which student would be selected to spend his junior year at an East Coast prep school in the United States.

In a strange way, Abaarso students have my miserable experience at Forest Grove Middle School to thank for their good fortune. Prior to Forest Grove, I was an excellent student at Flagg Street Elementary, a public school a few miles from my home. At Flagg Street, students respected teachers and the rules of the school. They wanted the teachers' approval, and they knew that approval came from being a good person and a caring student. I wasn't always the most disciplined student, and I was often in my own world doing my own thing, but most of Flagg Street's teachers appreciated me nonetheless.

I came to view Flagg Street as a model of what public education can achieve in K–6, whereas Forest Grove Middle School showed how quickly a bad school can destroy progress. In homeroom, the kids talked about how so-and-so got beaten up by this other kid in a fight after school, and

I'd think, "I don't want to be anywhere near them." I didn't know who "them" was, so I just avoided anyone I didn't know. By the time the school bus dropped me off each afternoon, I had no interest in thinking about school again until faced with it the next day, so I didn't do any homework. As one friend later described it, "At Forest Grove, it was cool to be dumb. I did my best to be cool."

Everything about Forest Grove demoralized me, but the final straw came at the end of one eighth-grade pre-algebra class, when our teacher passed back the graded exams. I saw that she had not seen one of my answers and therefore incorrectly marked it wrong. This was not necessarily her fault, since my handwriting was atrocious and my writing was all over the page. I brought it up to her to explain.

"I had the right answer there," I said, pointing to it.

She didn't even bother to check my work and see that I indeed had built up to the correct answer. "You just wrote it in," she nastily snapped, accusing me of cheating. My hatred of the school came to a hard boil. My teacher was baselessly attacking my integrity, the one thing I had kept through my two years in that colossal waste of taxpayer money.

That was it for me. From then on, I refused to grant Forest Grove even the slightest part of my mind and soul. That term, I received a D in math, formerly my best subject, and my mother knew something had to be done. Since my birth my parents had been saving money for me to go to college, but she said, "At the rate you are going, there isn't going to be any college." So my parents took those savings, negotiated whatever financial aid they could, and sent me to Worcester Academy, a prep school not far from my house, which was then around $10,000 per year for a day student.

Worcester Academy was founded in 1834. When I attended, the campus covered a city block in a tough part of Worcester. The class sizes were small, students and teachers generally respected each other, and performance was king, whether that was through academics, sports, or the arts. I thought the place was kind of stuffy, but in general I performed well there.

I graduated from Worcester Academy in 1994, glad to be done. I'm pretty sure the WA establishment felt the same way about me. While I'd recovered grade-wise, I was clearly still an underachiever. My ninth-grade math teacher privately told me, "You could be up there with the top kids;

you just don't try," and he was absolutely right. While I was no longer at Forest Grove, the damage it had done to me took years to heal.

In the decade-plus since I'd graduated, Worcester Academy had hired a new headmaster, Dexter Morse, who brought the school into the modern age and loosened up its stiff approach. As part of its progressive remake, it had begun an Open Gates program, which, in its own words, "integrated real-world experiences with the school's curriculum." Whole Child Education had come to Worcester Academy, which included affluent kids doing community service, and the administration decided to include Abaarso School in their projects. The students, led by my old class adviser, raised money and gathered supplies for our first container from the United States to Somaliland. Worcester Academy invited me to be a speaker for an Open Gates lecture series, "Global Problems: Obstacles and Opportunities," which gave me a chance to preach about my favorite topic of the time: "The Failure of Aid Work and NGOs in Africa." I also guest-taught a history class and Skyped in one of the Abaarso students, which made for a particularly terrific lesson. The WA students were engaged and took advantage of the opportunity to ask the types of questions you'll never find in books. Clan behavior was of particular interest, and they asked questions such as "Does each clan have a meeting place?" and "How do you know who your clansmen are?"

In a move that would have astounded my former teachers, most of whom probably grabbed old yearbooks to figure out who I was, Worcester Academy presented me with their Young Alumnus Award for founding Abaarso. It was nice to be welcomed home so warmly, and it led to conversations about all that was possible. It turned out a 1960s graduate of WA, Harry Emmons, had been in the armed forces in Africa and had endowed a scholarship for an African student to attend his alma mater. The thing about such a scholarship is that finding a qualified candidate is easier said than done. You can't just go to FindGreatAfricanStudents .com. The previous recipients of the scholarship had not always thrived, and one year they couldn't find a qualified African. The headmaster agreed to meet with me to see what we could work out.

Unlike me, Dexter Morse was the consummate headmaster, looking the part, bespectacled in a suit and tie. I was known to be on campus in my pajamas, with the *mawiis* skirt on top of them and sandals on my feet.

Sometimes, when teaching, I'd get caught up in the subject and not realize that my sandals were no longer on. Dexter was all for sponsoring an
Abaarso student, no doubt seeing the strategic fit of connecting one alum's
charitable gift with another alum's school. Still, there were doubts. "I'm
not saying I feel this way, but some here wonder if even the top student in
Somaliland can possibly compete at Worcester Academy," he told me.

There's no question that we'd have doubters everywhere until we
proved our worth. Abaarso has Dexter Morse and the sponsoring Emmons
family to thank for giving us that chance. Dexter agreed to fund one Abaarso
boy to come to the school for the following academic year. In addition,
WA would bring two girls to campus for their summer program.

Much of Somaliland had heard me promise to bring Somali children
to the United States to further their education, but to them it was so far-
fetched that it's hard to say how many believed me. One student actually
told me that it was a turnoff because he knew it was a lie. Well, now it is
going to happen, but the question is, who are we going to send?

The decision of whom to send is arguably the most important yet in
Abaarso's short history. It is our chance for proof of concept, and it has
come earlier than I had expected; scholarships to boarding schools were
not in my initial plans. An Abaarso student will spend the year at a nearly
two-century-old private school that is known by colleges across America. They don't know Abaarso, and they aren't coming to visit anytime
soon, but a Worcester Academy transcript is a proven commodity. If our
student performs well, he will show the world that Abaarso kids can compete. If the opposite happens, we might as well pack up our bags and go
home. Like colleges, boarding schools are now over $50,000 per year, and
people aren't going to cough up that kind of money if we strike out in
our first at bat.

Worcester Academy trusts me to make the decision, and I set up a
committee to screen the candidates and make recommendations. We
create an application, and students need to go through a formal process.
The students are thrilled, some referring to it as their dream opportunity, though a few are still a bit skeptical. Harry, our assistant headmaster,
reports one bizarre rumor that the plan is somehow a conspiracy
involving the Central Intelligence Agency and Coca-Cola.

Semifinalists are chosen, and they interview in front of the teachers, the boys competing for the full-year scholarship, and the girls for two spots in the summer program. Worcester Academy thought a Muslim girl might face specific challenges, so the summer program presented a chance to work through them. Nimo is fantastic in her interview, intelligent, thoughtful, and serious, but she is still underachieving in her courses. While I continue to think she hung the moon, many of the teachers are turned off by her lack of interest in their subjects. Deqa, the girl who'd almost given up on school, has been the best all-around Abaarso student from start to finish. She is my advisee, and I know her well. I certainly support her as a choice, as do many of the teachers after her interview.

One teacher wonders if Deqa would come back to Somaliland after being abroad. "Deqa, in many ways, life is easier in America," he puts forth. "Once you finish your education, don't you think you'll want to stay there?"

"America is a great developed country," Deqa responds. "America already has lots of doctors. Somaliland doesn't, so I need to come home and be a doctor here."

Selecting Deqa is a no-brainer. One girl down, one to go.

The application process is the first time I really get to know Fadumo Yusuf Abdilahi. Fadumo is intelligent, driven, and good-natured. While she will never threaten to reach five feet tall, she can laugh about herself, sometimes even signing off "Shorty Fadumo." She is one of eighteen children from her father's two wives, thirteen from her mother. She is number eight, with two older sisters and five older brothers. One of her older sisters had gone to study in Malaysia after high school, but her father had only let that happen because one of her brothers went as her chaperone. Fadumo had spoken to her sister often about schooling abroad, and that had become her dream, too. She doubted she would be allowed, however. Her father had said he would not send another girl. The expectation was that a girl would get married, but Fadumo has no interest in taking that path. She wants to be a doctor.

Fadumo had missed the Sheikh exam but then heard from a cousin that Abaarso was still accepting students. Her father is extremely strict and protective, and, like many Somalilanders, fears foreigners invading their culture and converting students to Christianity. He cares about his daughters and genuinely believes they need this type of safeguarding.

Fadumo had gone on a hunger strike, vowing not to eat until he allowed her to sit for our exam. Always thinking one step ahead, she had given his phone number for the acceptance results. He always got excited when one of his children received a good grade, so her strategy was that his excitement at her acceptance would be stronger than his resistance to letting her attend.

Fadumo had been a top scorer on our test. Nonetheless, her plan almost did not work. Yes, her father was happy that she got in, but he still had to be convinced to let her attend. We had certainly been excited when he agreed and glad to have her on board. Here at Abaarso, she is an academic star with grades just a smidgen below Deqa's. The two of them are so far ahead of the rest of the girls that it is theirs to lose, and far from losing it, they are both great in the interviews. So, Deqa and Fadumo become the two girls selected for the summer at Worcester Academy.

As far as the full year's scholarship is concerned, two boys stand out from the group, and I am happy to bet the school's future on either. In one corner is Mubarik, still working to overcome the English gap but dominating nonetheless. His analytical mind is absolutely superior. In the other is Mohamed, the picture of tenacity. He is so determined, so focused, that you know he will scrap his way to the elite of anywhere, just as he's done in Abaarso, going from the bottom five to the top five. I walk into the meeting completely neutral between the two. Then Tom, our math teacher since day one, expresses a strong vote for Mubarik. No one argues against it. Maybe others agree with Tom, or maybe, like me, they are neutral. But we have a winner.

Now the auditorium is hushed before the announcement: "Congratulations, Mubarik. You are going to America!"

I've never seen a group of people as happy for someone else as these students are for Mubarik. It must be something about Somalis, because I would see this kind of support for a fellow student often in the future. Watching the boys carry Mubarik on their shoulders is a moment I will never forget.

The irony, of course, is that Mubarik will be carrying all of them on his shoulders. Abaarso's future now entirely depends on this young nomad who'd arrived two years earlier with little education and without a word of English.

PART FOUR

THE GREAT MISCALCULATION

A fool and his money are soon parted.

—PROVERB

20

THE WHITE MAN
SPEAKS SOMALI

Just as the students are beginning to thrive, storm clouds are gathering on the horizon. Out of all the miscalculations I made in planning Abaarso, and there were many, none was bigger than my underlying assumption that the people would welcome me with open arms.

By any measure, what I was bringing to the community was huge. I had already donated $500,000 of my own money, a large donation even in the United States, and absolutely massive when applied to a country where the average wage is about $100/month. I had relocated my life to Somaliland and brought all my skills, my business contacts, and my energy. What I'd built was tangible, it was for their children, and I didn't take so much as a dollar of salary from the school. In fact, I was giving more money every day. Wouldn't the local population be thrilled to have me?

In reality it can't even be called a miscalculation, as it never occurred to me to even ask that question. I was so naive.

Somalilanders have little interaction with the outside world and a deep mistrust of foreigners' intentions. They are friendly and engaging, but they are suspicious of all newcomers.

My very first trip to Hargeisa's market, the *suuq*, was also my first chance to be in an authentic Somali setting. I went there with a woman

who was acting as my Somali guide. The *suuq,* which spanned the equivalent of about two city blocks, was a crowded maze of stalls. It was loosely
divided by the kind of merchandise for sale. A large section displayed
brightly colored fabrics stacked on tables and hanging from hooks.
Women could choose a fabric, then find one of the seamstresses in the
suuq to make them a traditional dress for $5. Another section sold T-shirts,
housewares, and trinkets that mostly come from China. I saw sneakers
that cost less than $10, but even that price seemed steep given their poor
quality. There were all kinds of items boasting famous brand names, but
they were obviously knockoffs. In the food section, some women manned
a table stacked with meat in the open air with no refrigeration or covering. I did not understand how this was okay, but there were buyers.
I bought one box of cereal labeled "Fruit Loops," wanting a taste of
home. The cereal was the wrong color and shape, and tasted like deter-
gent. The vegetables and fruits were limited to a few choices, mostly pota-
toes, tomatoes, onions, watermelons, and mangoes. The country had
limited agriculture, so the vast majority of the fresh food came from
deep within Ethiopia to the south.

Shopkeepers were eager to show me whatever they were selling, even
women's shoes. "*Galab Wannagsan,*" I said to one vendor as I walked by.
He paused for a second, in shock that I knew the Somali phrase for "Good
afternoon." With a big smile, he said "*Galab Wannagsan*" back to me,
then repeated "*Galab Wannagsan*" to the people around him, who started
saying it as well. There were almost no white people at the *suuq,* and
hardly any in Somaliland, so my presence was causing a stir, with people
talking and staring at me. When I asked my guide what they were saying,
she replied, "The white man speaks Somali!"

I was such a curiosity that a crowd formed to follow us. They were
pleased and far more welcoming because of my attempts at their language. That my Somali was extremely limited was both apparent and
irrelevant. The vendors and the shoppers cared that I had shown respect
for their ethnicity. Billeh has always said the Somali people don't care
about one race versus another; you are either ethnically Somali or you
aren't. They have great pride in their heritage.

From the outside, Somaliland looked the part of a society ripe for
international help, and I saw little to contradict this view. Somalilanders

were incredibly friendly people, in my opinion much more so than Americans or Europeans. They were particularly proud of their country and excited to put it on display.

It was easy to catch development fever hanging around the lobby of the Maansoor Hotel during my first visit to Somaliland. One Somali businessman was launching a ketchup factory. Other Somalis were talking about restarting the old Berbera cement factory. The projects would never happen, but I didn't know that.

Then there were the white folks in the lobby, NGO guys pounding away at their laptops. The big shot of this group was a German man who led the European Commission's mission to Somaliland. All the NGO folks kissed up to him because he controlled big wads of money. This could be the reason for his sizable ego. "You're talking about a couple hundred students? I'm talking about curing poverty!" he boasted to me, as if it were that simple.

Back then I had no understanding of how poorly these aid projects worked or how little the population expected from them. I had come here to open a top school for promising scholars, and the people of Hargeisa seemed so warm and welcoming that I envisioned clear sailing ahead. I didn't know how suspicious they were of any foreigners settling among them, and that the false promises of so many NGOs had reinforced this. The German leader would leave Somaliland, poverty would not, and I'm sure he was paid handsomely just the same. When my turn came to go from "tourist" to "foreigner on a mission" status, I would be up against all the difficult history that preceded me.

21

A COMPLEX WORLD

Before the Abaarso School took its name from the small village where it is located, the school was called Somaliland Academy of Science, but an early conversation I had with a Somali living in the United States changed that.

I had gone to eat at a Somali restaurant in Boston near a giant mosque. While it didn't look particularly Somali, it was a place Somalis could meet and eat like they were back home. The owner was a nice gentleman who upon learning I was planning to build a school in Somaliland came to sit with me. He said the site I had selected was a bad choice, as most Somalis would not feel welcome there. He thought his home village would be a better location. By how he described it, I thought it was in the eastern part of Somaliland.

"Oh, so you're from Somaliland?" I asked him.

"No, I'm from Somalia," he replied.

Next he showed me his village on the map, and now I was completely confused. "Isn't that Somaliland?" I inquired. The spot where he was pointing was definitely inside of the boundary of geographic Somaliland.

"No, it is Somalia," he insisted.

Now, I was truly baffled. "Does the government of Somaliland consider your homeland to be within its borders as part of the original British Somaliland?"

"Yes, it does," he replied.

"So it is Somaliland," I stated.

"No, it is Somalia."

This man's home village is east of the Somali city of Las Anod, well within the confines of the former British Somaliland, yet he clearly was not recognizing Somaliland's current independence. This was my first big lesson in Somali clan politics.

In Hargeisa, Somaliland patriotism is all around, the green, white, and red of the flag everywhere. I assumed that everyone from Somaliland was *for* Somaliland, but things aren't that simple. The restaurant owner was from an area within the former British protectorate, but he wasn't a member of Somaliland's dominant Isaaq clan, nor were most of the people who lived in that region. As far as he was concerned, his clansmen had joined with Somalia after independence in 1960, and there was no looking back. They had no interest in joining this "rebellion," which they felt cut them off from their larger clan, the majority of whom were outside the British Somaliland borders.

Perhaps the most interesting thing about the restaurant owner was that he had lived in Boston for decades, and I'm not sure he'd ever returned home in that time. Nonetheless, his clan loyalty was undiminished. He wasn't playing games with me or being difficult. His mind could not begin to consider "Somaliland" his home.

When I learned that not all people in Somaliland were pro–Somaliland independence, I thought it best to avoid politics. If I could start again, I might have kept the original name. But at that time, naming the school after the local village seemed like the safe play.

22

THE VILLAGE

Abaarso Village is little more than an assortment of shack-like shops on a half-mile stretch of the highway that runs from the border of Ethiopia to Somaliland's capital of Hargeisa. It is not a highway in the American sense, more a main road through a desolate stretch of desert, with goats rummaging among the rocks and scrub plants. Abaarso Village is only nine miles from the outer-city limit of Hargeisa, and it is home to a customs office that processes imports from Ethiopia. The shops sell drinks, packaged cookies, and *sambusas*, bite-size pastries stuffed with meat, to the passing travelers. That's about it in terms of commerce. The shops themselves look so flimsy that I wonder how they remain standing in an Abaarso wind.

Most of the dwellings in the village, which is along the main road, are makeshift. You see materials marked "UN" being used for roofing. Flattened tin cans have been nailed together to form aluminum walls. Other shelters are made of cloth propped up by sticks. There are not many concrete houses. There are small farms in the distance, but in this arid, inhospitable climate, the fields are only green in the rainy season.

The first weekend of school, I lead the students on the thirty-minute walk down to the village. We bring garbage pails with us and upon arriving start picking up the trash that is everywhere. The villagers' first reaction is anger. They think we are stealing their trash. Not that they want the trash for anything; in fact, they'd rather it get cleaned up. It is simply that no one has ever done something like this before, and they can't comprehend that we are truly there to help. There is absolutely no trust.

Periodically, students make the walk down to the village for tea and *sambusas*, which they eat at the plastic tables and chairs outside the shops. The boys are allowed to go to the village unchaperoned, but the girls need a teacher to escort them. On the occasions when male teachers walk the girls, the villagers make comments. We have to prod them to translate, as the comments are in Somali, but it is always some version of "Stay away from these white men," with an implication that we Westerners must have plans to harm Somali women.

The girls are rightfully embarrassed and at the time, of course, I am infuriated. Not only is it insulting, but it is also an injustice based on prejudice. There is no way they would say these things if our teachers were Somali men.

Before the staff and I arrived in Abaarso, most of the villagers had probably never seen a white person, not even on TV, as the village only recently received electricity. Some of them had never seen a non-Somali. They were completely unfamiliar with anything that was not Somali, and in this way they were like the vast majority of their countrymen. Somaliland used to be a British "protectorate," not a "colony," because the British only had a small interest in the area. It is thought that fewer than one hundred British were ever in the country, and almost all of them pulled out at independence in 1960. After the merger with Somalia, Mogadishu, five hundred miles to the south, became the dominant city in the country, not Hargeisa or any other city in the north. Mogadishu was the international city where all the foreigners stayed, while the former British Somaliland remained a mostly rural and nomadic society.

When I first arrived in Somaliland, a security expert told me that there were fewer than fifty Westerners in the country, and I'd already learned that those people were not interacting with the actual society. Mostly they were hopping between secured compounds meeting with bigwigs and writing reports.

Like the nomadic Mubarik thinking a truck was an animal, the villagers had no framework to approach what they were seeing at the school. They only knew that it looked and acted different, which made them uncomfortable and put them on the defensive. It is not that different from when a first black family would move into an all-white town in the United States. People often believe the worst until they are convinced otherwise.

23

LIKE WATER THROUGH
A SIEVE

It is spring 2010, an ordinary afternoon in our first year at Abaarso, and I'm called to the front gate to handle a problem. The security at school is supposed to be tight, with both SPUs, Special Protection Units, and watchmen. We have about a dozen watchmen on staff, and they are gathered together. I notice one in particular who must be six foot six and has a menacing look. I have a translator with me so we can communicate.

The watchmen aren't alerting me to a problem they've seen; the watchmen are the problem.

"You will immediately double all of our pay and cover all of our medical expenses," the chosen speaker announces.

"Or else?" I ask.

"Or we all quit and leave right now."

"So you will quit in the middle of a shift and leave the school without your protection?"

"You must double our pay and cover all our medical expenses."

I don't need to think for a second before responding. Luckily, my translator probably doesn't know the Somali for "Don't let the door hit you on the way out."

NGOs had convinced the local population that foreigners were gullible, deep pocketed, and not going to do anything useful anyway. To a local living on tiny wages, he might as well get what he can. That's how the villagers no doubt saw us in these early days. They had no idea if this compound on the hill would ever improve their lives, but what they did think was that we had a lot of money. They weren't used to a situation where the guy who controlled the money was also the guy whose money it was. That isn't how most nonprofits work. Normally, there's the head of the organization in Somaliland who reports to Nairobi who reports to D.C., who, after several more steps down the line, reports to the taxpayer. The taxpayer isn't even aware that Somaliland exists, never mind that he's paying for some program there. NGOs are nongovernmental organizations, but they do take government funding. It's just that the government doesn't run them. But unlike the American taxpayers, who don't know they are getting robbed, I did know, and every shortfall at the school would come out of my pocket. People were trying to overcharge us for everything, and it aggravated me that villagers considered our school to be their piggy bank.

I was beginning to realize that I could no longer rely much on Khadar to negotiate these kinds of issues, despite his Somaliland expertise. He had been our partner on the ground while I was setting things up from the United States. We created a Somaliland entity with Billeh as chairman, Khadar as vice chairman, and me as the chief executive, for which I used the finance term "managing director." The board, however, had never taken on its proper role of oversight and assistance, with Khadar instead periodically sticking his head in and acting on his own. When I was in the United States this was necessary, but now we should have been running professionally.

Despite his confidence and local knowledge, Khadar was unhelpful when it came to running a tight ship, which I chalked up to his history as a politician who wants everyone to like him. I didn't realize that virtually everyone I was dealing with was his clansman, no doubt another reason he didn't want to take a hard line. His clansmen would expect his loyalty to them, not to some foreigners.

Before moving onto the Abaarso campus, Khadar insisted we put the kitchen in the northwest corner of the campus five hundred feet from the cafeteria, down a steep hill. In fact, the kitchen was forty feet lower in altitude than the cafeteria. He said he and the new cook, who was, of course, one of Khadar's relatives, didn't want the smell to be near the students, so it needed to be done this way. I thought this was ridiculous and said so. How could the smell be so bad that it would justify such a setup? I couldn't figure out why they were pushing this, but Khadar fought hard, insisting this was the right way to do things in Somaliland. Eventually, I decided this wasn't worth fighting with Khadar. What was the worst that could happen? We soon saw part of the answer: the meals were disasters. Due to the kitchen's location, the vats of rice and other mass-produced food had to be rolled up a hill that was not only steep but incredibly rocky. It was so difficult that we often had to put the food into a car and drive it up. This required our car to be on campus, which was not always possible. So of course, the meals were rarely served on time. How was this the better way?

Our method for serving the meals was also terrible. All fifty kids would line up in the cafeteria, as the head cook insisted on personally spooning out food one student at a time. There were others to help and multiple lines could have formed, but the head cook seemed to insist on some sort of ritual. First, the cook would receive the plate, then scoop some rice on it, then scoop some sauce on the rice, then maybe add a lime or a spicy Somali topping called *shigney*. It would take forever to serve each student, and those in the back of the line were rightfully annoyed.

The head cook for the kids was a tall, thin, older man whom Khadar suggested I hire. He stated that the magnitude of the job required that he have more manpower, which it probably did. He brought on four other men from the village—all clansmen of his and Khadar's—to help him in the kitchen, which for fifty students was more manpower than necessary. They were hired before I knew what had happened, so now I would have to fire some of them, which created more trouble than not hiring them in the first place. This was offensive to my sense of efficiency, not to mention bad for the budget, but I would have to wait to address the situation later. We had a more pressing concern.

There was significant inventory loss happening in the kitchen. As the kitchen itself had been placed in the far corner of campus, our outer wall

paralleled two of its sides. As extra defense against intruders, the wall
had glass on top; however, the glass was not sharp and could easily be
removed by hand. You didn't even need to do it carefully, so the glass in
fact provided no physical defense at all. One day early on, I saw that a
section of glass a few feet long had been removed from the wall directly
behind the kitchen. This was a section of the wall that the kitchen completely blocked from view. I alerted the handyman, a villager named
Mohamoud who had previously been the construction company's watchman for the site. He took some cement and put the glass back in the
wall. The next time I looked, the glass was gone again, and again Mohamoud repaired the wall. When it happened a third time, I knew something deliberate was going on. Sacks of flour, sugar, and rice were being
smuggled over the wall. The kitchen's location offset its difficulty of operations with its ease of theft. Perhaps why it was put there?

Keeping track of the school's assets was like keeping water in a sieve.
All kinds of resources were leaking out of the campus. I watched women
from the village fill up their yellow water jugs at our tanks and then walk
out to bring them home. The head cook was right there and was at least
accepting of it, if not outright inviting it. Our guards either didn't consider this an important issue, or maybe even thought I was okay with it,
or they were watchmen from the village, whose loyalties lay with the villagers. Mohamoud, the man who fixed the glass, was genuinely honest,
but that didn't mean he was going to stand in their way. It was one
thing to quietly replace the missing glass but another to forcibly block
his clansmen.

I thought about the water jugs and the fact that Abaarso was a poor
village that struggled with the cost of water. But this was not our mission. We weren't an NGO focused on water. As was true with the villagers, our water needed to be trucked in, and we couldn't possibly solve
all of the problems in their society. People were testing the boundaries,
and if we didn't tighten up, the floodgates would open. We'd need to
block off all leaks, whether they be theft, waste, or unnecessary staffing.
I ran out to block any yellow jugs from leaving, I talked to the cook, I
talked to the guards, and I even permanently blocked off a second exit
from the campus that I couldn't monitor. This was one step in the strug-

gle for efficiency, a victory Abaarso needed for survival but one that was not without its costs. I had made a number of local people mad.

First, I didn't act like a Somali; then I didn't act like a salaried NGO worker who had no incentive to stop such graft. At this point, the villagers considered me the worst of both worlds; I am not Somali and I am not a pushover. They are used to non-Somalis at least being easy marks.

24

DOING SOMETHING RIGHT

When you don't understand people, you have no idea about the many ways you might be upsetting them. You are also surprised when you finally do something right.

Our auditorium is a large concrete structure with a sizable stage and granite-tiled floors that slope upward in several levels. Khadar had insisted on building it, saying it would bring revenue-generating conferences to campus. It seemed reasonable enough but turned out to be completely incorrect; the auditorium never brought a single dollar of income. The funds to build it were to come from a British government grant and a Somali donor. However, Khadar unilaterally changed the designs, which added significantly to the cost. I wasn't aware until I got the bill, and once again I needed to personally cover the shortfall.

Today villagers fill our auditorium in order to sign their young children up for afternoon classes at Abaarso. It is chaotic, but that is because of the excitement. The villagers are bringing their kids to Abaarso; the school is now for them, too.

It has now been fourteen months since we arrived at Abaarso. The public school is about halfway between our school and the village itself. From the beginning, we'd been sending our students to teach there.

Some days, Deqa, Amal, Nimo, and other students had taught English. Other days, a group of boys had taught math and Arabic. They would walk down with me or another teacher. The program needed improvement, but it had been a way to help the community. However, it turned out that the full-time teachers in the village school considered the program competitive, sometimes even telling us we couldn't come. That is one reason we are now moving the classes to our campus.

For the life of me, I cannot understand why the village is now excited about the after-school program on our campus, when they hadn't seemed to care about the same program at their school. Maybe it is seen as a gesture that we are willing to share? Maybe they think that the secret to education is the facility itself? Our classrooms are certainly nicer and our fields great for playing. Whatever their reason, I hadn't predicted their positive reaction any more than I'd predicted their initial mistrust.

The move to our campus makes for a massive improvement, and not just for the unexpected PR. We'd had a hard time teaching the kids in their own classrooms. There, they had come to behave in a certain way. We were the visitors and subject to their rules of engagement. Now, in our environment, the children are open to our way of doing things. This means properly behaving and following the discipline code. The program is also now far easier for our teachers to manage.

Our students have learned so much from these "student-teacher" experiences. It has helped Amal, whose struggles with math had left her in serious need of a confidence boost. For Nimo, it is a new passion, her own schooling having still not inspired her. At times, she puts more effort into these classes than her own. And for all our students, it shows them what it is like to be on the other side of the desk. Periodically, our students become incensed that some of those kids had dared to "cheat on my test!"

While education levels in Somaliland are generally very low, there is still a giant gap between schooling in Hargeisa and in a rural place like Abaarso Village. In the latter, there are scores of people who are completely illiterate. We've had documents on which villagers need to sign their name, but only a couple can, so the rest have to use a fingerprint instead. Some of the kids who come to the after-school program do not even know the alphabet.

A couple of years into the new program, we are ready to let some Abaarso Village students sit for our entrance exam. When the exam is over, we accept the top-scoring student, a girl named Juweriya, whose father owns a qat shop on the main drag. More villagers follow her in the next years, and they manage to hold their own. More village children show up each afternoon. They hope to get into Abaarso one day—or at least receive some education even if they don't. The future of the village is looking brighter, and with that comes improved relations.

Economists use the idea of "revealed preferences," in which the actions of people reveal how they truly feel. For example, some might say they don't like McDonald's, but if they eat there twice a week, they have "revealed" that they really do like it. So what can we make of the villagers sending their children to school at Abaarso? These were the same people who once warned our girls that we were out to do them harm. While I wouldn't kid myself that the Abaarso staff and the villagers are now best of friends, one has to conclude that both sides have come a long way. We may not fully understand each other, but there's one thing we know for sure: we all care about the well-being of their children.

25

MONEY DISGUISED
AS RELIGION

Unfortunately, not all our local problems are due to ignorance. Abaarso School had its enemies before we even opened our doors. Private for-profit schooling is a big business in Somaliland, and while some, like Young Muslim Academy, are supportive of our effort, others consider us a threat. Rumors are rampant, and many of our parents are under attack for sending their girls to be with the "infidels." Some say we are missionaries and that we are out to do harm. When our students go back home on weekends or school breaks, they hear heckling in town from people who know nothing about Abaarso. Some even get in physical fights with those spreading these lies.

The heads of their former schools are the worst offenders.

"I hear they're trying to change your religion."

"No, that hasn't happened at all."

"How do you know? They might be doing it in a secret way."

Anyone who has met a missionary knows they are neither coy nor fans of playing the long game. Anyone who knows me knows I have no interest in religion. These accusers don't care, as *they* are the ones with the secret agenda. Such attacks are not unprecedented. SOS is a European organization, and when they first reopened the Sheikh School, they faced many of the same rumors. Those proved baseless, and by the time

I'd arrived, SOS was considered the top school in Somaliland, but that doesn't stop the attackers from trying again. In business terms, for-profit competitor schools exploit religious and cultural fears to create a barrier to entry.

One of our students' mother told me the following story. She had gone to discuss a problem with the headmistress of the school where her younger children are enrolled. But instead of the school addressing her concern, the headmistress attacked her. "Your girls at Abaarso are having their religion changed," she scolded. She had never set foot on our campus, but five of her former students were now at Abaarso, which meant lost revenue.

The maligning of Abaarso is hard for the students and parents alike. It also creates additional security concerns. After all, it has only been six years since the brutal assassination of the British couple who came to Somaliland to reopen the Sheikh School under SOS's auspices. Attacks based on religion, no matter how unfounded, put our teachers in danger. No walls, especially ones with removable glass fragments, could keep one safe from a society that turned against you. Our guards are local people, and with enough bad rumors, even they could quickly become enemies.

26

TROUBLE WITH THE BOYS

Within the school, we are constantly dealing with gender issues. Somaliland boys aren't used to the competitive role of the female in the classroom setting. I have seen it myself; girls at other schools take a backseat in education, lacking the role models and support the boys receive. In fact, Deqa had been the only girl to score in the top 25 on our entrance exam with SOS. Now the Abaarso boys, accustomed to their gender roles, are watching girls compete against them and even surpass them in many ways. While some appreciate the girls' achievement, others feel threatened.

How each boy views the issue seems to directly correlate with how he is faring in the transition to Abaarso. Boys like Mohamed and Mubarik are too busy trying to excel to worry about how the girls are doing. For others who aren't finding it easy, the new world order has knocked them a bit off-kilter. I'm not even sure they can explain what it is that is bothering them, but they know something is wrong. By far the worst offender is a boy we'll call Shakib. He isn't picking up English quickly, and while he had come in with one of the higher math scores, he struggles to shift to our critical-thinking-driven classes. It seems to me that he wants someone to feel superior to, and with students surpassing him in the classroom, that someone is getting hard to find.

Not that I necessarily help the situation. I know that most of the boys believe they are smarter than the girls. Our boys need to see them as equals, and I am quite aggressive in making sure they see with their own eyes what the girls are capable of. When Nimo comes up to the whiteboard with her Dragon Problem answer, I call out, "Nimo's on the second problem. Is anyone else even close?" It is a bit obnoxious, but I can't help myself. Sometimes I go even further. "I thought all boys were smarter than girls," I chide them. "Doesn't seem like it." They get my point, and the most resistant don't like it one bit.

Not long into our first year, a small group of boys, led by Shakib, lashes out. Like the for-profit schools that insult Abaarso, these boys choose religion as their point of attack. Shakib all but declares himself to be the "commissioner of the religious police," and quickly many of the boys fall in line behind him. It doesn't take me long to realize a clear dynamic in the school; everyone is terrified that they will be labeled as "not religious enough" by this self-appointed "commissioner" and his panel. Shakib has essentially seized power.

One of the first clues that awakens me to the religious posturing occurs in a meeting with the students after showing them a film. I thought showing movies would be a fun way to hear and learn English, while also learning about the world. As we are in Africa, I decide to show *Hotel Rwanda*, the story of a hotel manager named Paul Rusesabagina, who gives refuge to a thousand persecuted Tutsi tribesmen during the Hutu militia's siege in Rwanda. It is a good movie with a powerful message.

The day after the movie, we hold an assembly. I ask the kids if they liked it. One of the Abdis replies, "We liked it, Teacher, we liked it, but there was something in this movie that was against our religion."

"The genocide of innocent people?" I ask, certainly hoping that is the answer.

Dismissing that, he refers to the part where the husband and wife characters kiss. "We know Rwandan men and women kiss, but we are not really supposed to see that."

Abdi is referring to the scene where Paul, the main character, and his wife are on the roof of the hotel, and he tells her that if the hotel gets invaded, she should gather their children on the roof and together they will jump to their deaths. "The machete is no way to die," Paul tells her, after which he kisses her. It is not a sexual kiss in any fashion, but rather a solemn kiss of what could be a "good-bye."

If a vote were taken for "least religious student on campus," I'm quite sure this particular Abdi would win. If it were an anonymous election, he'd even vote for himself. Yet his public response about the film shows that each and every student fears for his or her religious reputation, and fear is exactly what the so-called religious police will use.

Which is not to say Abdi is wrong. From then on, we will not let the students see anything that can be considered remotely romantic. We screen every movie first and time how far into the film each potentially offensive scene occurs. Right before a "censored" scene, we pause the film and cover the projector with a sheet. The most ridiculous part is that every time we do this, a bunch of kids boo, showing just how confused they are. Eventually, we take the further step of having the boys and girls view movies separately.

Another issue arises when I coach the Abaarso girls at basketball. Many of the girls have never participated in gym before. A few others have, and have even been taught sports by a male coach. That first year, I am the only adult on campus who knows how to coach basketball, and some of the girls have expressed an interest in the sport. The girls play dressed from head to toe with multiple layers, but nonetheless, Shakib, the thorn in my side, makes it an issue, saying it is inappropriate for males to be coaching the girls. Eventually, I stop. The girls aren't happy about this, insisting there is no religious basis for me not to be their coach. "If a Somali school has a male coach, why can't we?" they ask.

"Because we aren't a Somali-run school and I'm not Somali," I tell them. "Get used to the double standard." This fight isn't worth having. I'd never accept the girls getting an inferior education. If I thought I was compromising on that issue, I'd fight it hard. But none of them is going to the Women's National Basketball Association, so getting exercise is enough.

Shakib doesn't stop there, however. He and his group begin voicing opposition to male teachers spending time helping female students, though they don't say a word about boys spending time with female staff.

Religious belief is just a disguise in this case; it is not the true root of this rebellion. If Shakib were actually pious, then we wouldn't have caught him blatantly cheating.

The situation comes to a head when a reporter from the United States wants to interview our students. I arrange for five of them, three girls and two boys, to go to Hargeisa to meet with her. The boys are very late getting to the bus, and I don't want to miss the reporter, so we leave without them. The reporter meets us at the Maansoor Hotel and interviews the girls. Coincidentally, this is the same night that Ahmed Mohamed Mohamoud Silanyo wins the presidential election, and the victory is announced in a press conference held at the Maansoor. This turns the hotel into a mob scene, and it is hard for us to get out. The bus gets back as best it can, but not until ten or eleven that night.

The next day, a large group of boys tell me they need to meet with me. Of course, they are led by the self-appointed "commissioner" of what has become Abaarso's religious police. In front of all the boys, Shakib points a finger in my face and scolds, "You will not spend time with the girls!" *You will not this, and you will not that.* Another boy chimes in. "How do we know you were where you say you were?" he challenges. "Prove it!"

But the "commissioner" and some of his deputies aren't done. They persist until I call all the boys to the lecture hall for a meeting. Once again, Shakib points his finger in my face making demands, and this time I've had enough. "Here's the deal," I say. "I'm leaving the room right now and so are all of you. If you come back here in fifteen minutes, then I'll assume you want to be part of my school and that you will be students. You will never be so disrespectful to a teacher again. If not, the gate is open and all of you are welcome to leave. I'll just make Abaarso an all-girls' school."

Every boy comes back to the lecture hall, and the direct confrontations eventually come to an end. Shakib continues his reign of terror over the student body, but eventually he and other troublemakers will leave Abaarso; almost all are students who have struggled to perform. The boys and girls are equally thrilled to see Shakib go.

I realize this story paints an unfairly poor picture of the boys, who, like all the students, are growing up. One can't judge them on this behavior any more than we can judge students for initially cheating. In time, the boys become great supporters of the girls. It takes a while, but they come to see the girls as sisters and applaud the girls' successes as victories for all of Abaarso and even Somaliland. They also come to see that the teachers care as much about them as about the girls, so rather than fighting the positive teacher-girl relations, they should just develop their own strong connections with the staff.

As I often remind myself, no one ever said I'd be handed a glossy finished product. The point of education is to help the raw material grow into something special, and that's exactly what is happening. We are building something special, and we are all in it together.

27

KHADAR'S RAGE

In late July 2011, just days after the completion of our second school year, Khadar Ali drives his car to the middle of campus, throws open the passenger door, and steps out in a rage. He is angry and wants it to be known. He's driven through the gate as if he owns the place, which is no surprise. He is now yelling at my students, many of whom are outside when he arrives.

"It is my school! It is my school!" he rages, right in front of all of them.

"What makes it your school?" I ask.

"I built the wall!" he responds, referring to his oversight of construction of the cement security wall that encircles the school.

"With my money," I shoot back.

He then strides over to a group of boys and starts telling them that they should be angry, too, because this school favors girls. He tries to get my guards to arrest me, but to their credit, they want no part of any of this. When Khadar gets back in his car, he is still furious. As he speeds away, another man with him in the vehicle repeatedly shouts out the window at our girls, "Get the fuck off our land!"

Up until recently, Khadar had been problematic, but he'd also brought clear value to Abaarso. From the start, he seemed eager to be part of my plans and acted as "our Somali partner." He was extremely knowledgeable and connected in Somaliland, and he had been instrumental in the land acquisition for the school, when unbeknownst to me, he'd led us to his subclan's land. One of his strongest assets had been his contacts within the British Foreign Commonwealth Office. They told him about their desire to fund some educational initiatives in Somaliland, and he suggested to me that I write a proposal for Abaarso, with his own NGO, which we will call DEV, acting as the intermediary organization. While DEV acts solely in Somaliland, it is still legally an international NGO, so the British could send the money to DEV, who'd then give it to Abaarso. We were eventually awarded the grant, £150,000, the equivalent of about $225,000, over two years, which made me ecstatic. It seemed to be clear evidence that in Khadar I had found the right Somali partner.

Given my background and ultimate desire to attract donors, I wanted to ensure that our financial management was handled correctly from the start. I wasn't yet in Somaliland, so I relied on Khadar to disperse the funds I sent. Khadar agreed that he'd keep Abaarso funds separate from DEV rather than commingling funds. That way, we could easily match accounting to actual movements in money. But in time I realized this never happened and the monies remained commingled in his DEV account. The most generous explanation for this is carelessness. The least is not pretty. Unfortunately, this was the first, but by no means the last, financial management issue that arose between Khadar and Abaarso. In fact, it had been two years, and despite promises, he'd still never provided an accounting explanation for the first $10,000 I'd sent.

Bringing the school to Abaarso Village had convinced many people in the area that Abaarso was his school. Why else would the school be located in Abaarso? Why would anyone else go out of their way to put a school in that undeveloped village with no water or power? There was also the matter of the sign he'd posted at the building site while I was away in the States. The Abaarso School of Science and Technology sign said "Sponsored by DEV," with no mention of my having actually funded the construction. Whether Khadar had purposely made such oversights, or they were all accidents, one thing was for sure—much of the Somali world had come to believe that Khadar owned the school and his actions had supported this view.

People believing this false position had surely garnered Khadar clout, but I can only imagine that it also put him in challenging positions. When the watchmen demanded that I double their pay and I refused, many probably went to Khadar to say, "Khadar, you're the owner. Get me my job back." That's speculation, but based on Somaliland culture, it is an awfully reasonable one. Similarly, a parent of an expelled student might ask him to get his kid back in. In both cases, Khadar could make up a little story about how that white boy was behaving poorly, and he would fix it, but in time, people would see that Khadar didn't have the power he claimed. Over time, this would dig a deeper and deeper hole. He could come clean, but what if he could instead take over the school? Or just as effective, what if it completely collapsed? Couldn't he ultimately blame the failure on me, and no one would need to know that he wasn't really who they thought he was?

Over the past few months, our relationship has been unraveling. I've also heard that he's been badmouthing me and the school, even telling people that a fight is coming. There have been some attempts at negotiating our disagreements. Up until a week ago, it seemed we were close to a resolution. The parents had tried to reconcile us. My assistant headmaster, Harry, and two other teachers had also tried. Everyone wanted to let him save face in return for a written guarantee that he would not interfere with management or bother the school. But the Somalilanders, the ultimate mediators, had come back and told me that nothing could be accomplished. Khadar's sights were set on taking over the school. I had involved the school board's executive committee, showing them the financial issues, which included our missing a large chunk of money due from DEV for the British government grant. I showed them his governance violations, in which he acted like Abaarso's owner instead of just as a board member. For my relationship with Khadar, this had made things worse, significantly upping the ante and no doubt embarrassing him. But I didn't see much choice, considering he'd been ducking my requests for the accounting information for months, promising he'd send it right away and then never doing so.

When Khadar had finally sent some financials, they were fraught with inaccuracies, including double counting some items and putting too high a number on others. The math still had him owing the school about $30,000. He agreed to meet in person to discuss it but then canceled a few minutes before, when I was already in Hargeisa. By this time, I'd had enough and demanded that he meet me at once.

That's when all my fears came true. "Jonathan, you will leave the country immediately," he demanded. "The teachers will leave with you, and you can take the students, too." He concluded with, "You are on my land." After months of Khadar denying this was his intention, it was at least a relief to have his position out in the open.

Now, here he is on campus making a scene. The students stare in disbelief, unsure what they are witnessing. I'm too angry to be bewildered.

Before this step, Khadar had made mistakes, but he still could have maintained his reputation as a respected contributor to a great new school. Sure, he'd dug himself a hole, and people would learn that he didn't own Abaarso, but he could have called that an innocent misunderstanding. With the school's success, the Somali community would be congratulating everyone involved, and Khadar would have been a big part of that. What's more, he would have been a benefactor to his countrymen, as well as his clansmen, whose village hosts the school. Unfortunately, that's not the direction he took.

The day after his visit to campus, the gang of villagers shows up at the school's gate telling Harry they will kill me if I don't leave the country. A parent visiting campus even hears one of them saying they are going to turn the school and the campus into a hotel. Since the school had opened, nothing like this had ever occurred, and suddenly it happens right after Khadar has ordered me out of the country? I don't need to think hard to know who is behind our unwelcome visitors.

The future of Abaarso is now in question. In the world I come from, this has an easy solution. It's not Khadar's land, nor is it the village's land. The land belongs to the school. What's more, the students, parents, teachers, and largest funders are unequivocally behind me, and they want the school protected from Khadar. Legally, Khadar has no claim. He is only a board member, and short of a board vote to send the teachers, the students, and me home, he has no legal grounds whatsoever. But, of course, we are not in the world I come from. We are in a clan justice system in Khadar's subclan's territory. I am not from that subclan or any other. I am not even Somali. We are huge underdogs.

28

NOTHING IS EASY

For the next two weeks I am dealing with nothing but this problem. I go to see Somaliland's president, who promises to help, but after the visit I am forced to stay in Hargeisa, supposedly for my own safety. School is closed for the summer, and I am leaving to take my students to the United States for their scholarships at Worcester Academy.

Sadly, a few days before we leave, there is a delay in Fadumo's visa processing, and she can't go with us. She is devastated, and I am for her. We are beginning to understand the visa process, which is not easy for Somalis. There is no U.S. embassy in Somaliland or Somalia, and the United States has no formal diplomatic relations with either. Therefore, anyone trying to travel to the United States must go in person to the U.S. embassy in Djibouti.

Early in the morning of August 5, 2011, Mubarik, Deqa, and I take a bus to Berbera Airport. I dread most long trips, but today I am fueled by the excitement of watching my travel companions as they discover a whole new world. While my frustration with Khadar continues to weigh on my mind, for now I focus on the success of my kids.

The short flight from Berbera to Dubai is the first time Deqa and Mubarik have been on a jet plane, their flights to and from Djibouti having been flown on an ancient Soviet propeller plane. They are excited, but it is Dubai International Airport that really wows them. One could say Dubai International is a microcosm of all that is Dubai, but there is really nothing "micro" about it. A full assault on one's senses, it's a cross between Disneyland and Las Vegas—glitzy, gilded, and filled with huge displays of the fanciest cars and most desirable shops. It isn't just the size and luxury, or the ceilings, which are taller than any building in Somaliland; it is also the incredible range of people— well-heeled Europeans on vacation; American businessmen in Western suits; Arabic women fully covered, with just slits in their gold face masks; immigrants struggling with children and baggage. Among the shops, there are rooms for prayer, one for men and one for women. More international travelers go through Dubai than any other airport in the world, and its central location means they are off to India, the Pacific Islands, the Middle East, Africa, Europe, and even stops throughout the Americas. Our flight would be serviced by British Airways the whole way, changing planes in London.

Once at the airport in Dubai, Deqa and Mubarik see a world they could not have imagined existed. Deqa is so excited by what surrounds her that she declares, "I could stay here forever." She adds, "I love Dubai and I'm excited to see London next." Explaining that this is not really Dubai and our stopover at Heathrow would not really be London isn't worth bringing her down.

"I don't understand something, though. Who owns this?" she asks.

"Who owns what?" I ask, unsure of what she is referring to.

"Who owns this airport?"

In Somaliland, pretty much everything is owned by someone. Dahabshiil Money Transfer is owned by Mohamed Saeed Duale and his son Abdirashid, the Maansoor is owned by Abdulkadir Hashi, the Ambassador Hotel by Khadar Adan, and so on. Dubai Airport comprises a larger project than constructing all of Hargeisa, and Deqa cannot imagine anyone being rich enough to build it. Seeing a world of mass structures sparks questions she couldn't have previously conceived of, just as my coming to Somaliland has made me rethink assumptions. I explain in simple terms the concept of pooling funds through large corporations and government projects. I am not sure it all clicks, but Deqa seems captivated.

We sit down in one of the airport coffee shops for tea and hot chocolate. For the first of what will be about twenty times, I check them for their passports. Deqa is pure fascination, but Mubarik has a different reaction. Despite the whipped cream on his hot chocolate, he looks depressed. "It is hard to find out that everything you thought was good was really nothing," he states, obviously comparing Somaliland's limited development to what is here. The boy who a decade earlier had learned that a truck was not an animal is struggling with the latest shock.

I am enjoying my students' wonder right up until it is time to board our flight to London. We are halted in the boarding area by a British Airways representative, who puts me on the phone with someone from the British government. This person tells me that Deqa and Mubarik will not be allowed to board the flight.

"They have perfectly valid U.S. visas," I protest.

"We know that, and we don't question that," the official says. "But we don't recognize the Somalia or Somaliland passport. They can't come to England."

"They don't want to come to England," I argue. "They just want to transit from one British Airways flight to another in Heathrow Airport. They have scholarships in the United States."

My pleading doesn't have any effect. "It doesn't matter. They can't board" is the final answer. And with that we are stranded.

On the inside I am quite unhappy and nervous. It doesn't help that I haven't slept in forty-eight hours, a lot of the sleep deprivation on account of Khadar. As far as I am concerned, there is no good reason to deny entry to Mubarik and Deqa when they are obviously headed to something better than Heathrow Airport. I have no idea how many countries will block our entry, even though our final destination is the United States.

Not wanting to take any more risks, I decide we need to fly directly to the United States, to whichever city it might be. I look at the options online and see that there are direct flights to San Francisco, Houston, and New York. A New York flight has just closed, but another will be departing in eight hours. I rush to the ticketing line, Mubarik and Deqa in tow. I am trying to appear calm, not wanting to ruin their experience or worry them. Even before I reach the counter, I learn that there are five seats left on the flight, which leaves no time for delay. But there is still a complication. We are traveling on different itineraries, with Mubarik staying in the States for one year, and Deqa and I for a shorter time, meaning I cannot book all of our seats at once. *What if after I book Mubarik, the other seats get scooped up before I have a chance to book Deqa and me?* If that happens, Mubarik will have to figure out how to get from New York to Worcester on his own.

Then comes the next glitch. My credit card company blocks the purchase, for which I don't blame them. They should be suspicious, seeing my itinerary change mere hours before takeoff. Getting the authorization is hard. I don't have a phone that works in Dubai, so I borrow one and try to reach customer service. Finally, an agent picks up, and he authorizes Mubarik's flight first, then Deqa's and mine. I remain uneasy, wondering what other challenges await us. I hadn't expected to lose Fadumo in the visa issuance fiasco or be unable to change planes at a British airport, either—all lessons that prove it isn't easy to be a Somali trying to get to the United States.

As soon as the plane is in the air, I feel great relief, as I was silently waiting for someone to escort us off the flight. Every flight attendant who walked by made me nervous. I'm now overtired and almost delirious, but I don't sleep more than thirty minutes during the fourteen-hour flight, worrying about what is to come at Homeland Security. When we land and approach border control, my fears are realized when an officer tells Mubarik to follow him to a back area. Then, Deqa, too, is instructed to follow the officer. At first, I wait for them to reappear. But as it becomes clear that this is not going to resolve quickly, I ask if I could join them and am surprised to be let through. I find Mubarik and Deqa sitting on chairs, waiting to be called. No one has talked to them yet. They are tired and resigned that they have no control over anything going on. I still maintain the illusion that I have some.

At the desk, I ask why they are being delayed, and a nice gentleman explains, "They need extra processing, but the system is down. No telling how long it will be." Eventually, they are summoned and, without too much fuss, allowed entry. As we pass through the doors to where families await, I realize they can't stop us now. My first kids are officially in the United States! That I haven't slept in days, we are in New York and not Boston, and we now learn Mubarik's luggage is lost are small-time, solvable problems.

Despite my relief, I can't help but wonder why Mubarik and Deqa needed to go to border control in the first place. Their visas are in order, so being detained for extra screening seems unnecessary. It reminds me of how suspicious the Somalis are of me. We in the West have certainly had more interaction with those of other cultures, but we are still anxious and afraid of the unfamiliar.

Just being in a new society will teach Mubarik and Deqa so much. I am learning so much, too, even if it is the hard way.

29

HARRY'S MAD DASH

Harry sends me an e-mail. His communication reads:

> It has become clear to me that [a Ministry of Education official] is actively trying to stop Abaarso from receiving entry visas for its new teachers.

I am back home in Massachusetts, having turned Mubarik and Deqa over to their new educators at Worcester Academy. It's nice to be back with my mother in my childhood home. She provides some grounding in what is an otherwise awful time. I fear for Abaarso's very survival and the urgent e-mail from Harry Lee is a big part of that.

Harry had been completely new to education when he came to Abaarso in our second year. But he has been a great fit from the start. Intensely logical and analytic, he sees both the big picture and the fine details in a way that few people do. Harry was born in northern Nigeria, lived briefly in the United States, then moved to Cairo when he was four. His mother was in the Peace Corps and his father was in the Foreign Service. Harry was two years out of the University of Virginia when he joined Abaarso.

His e-mail refers to a problem we've been having with Immigration.

The situation has become so combustible that we are not even sure if our incoming teachers will be allowed to enter the country. Indeed, Harry is right about the visas being blocked. The official from Education has gone to the Ministry of the Interior, which oversees immigration, to tell him that visas are not to be issued for our incoming teachers. Harry protests to the official on the school's behalf, but for weeks the man keeps inventing excuses, including one about not being able to get into his e-mail account.

Harry's e-mail continues:

It's extremely frustrating and draining to work non-stop, without salary, to provide this country with a service while someone in the government does everything possible to obstruct our work. . . . We urgently need someone to intervene so he does not destroy our school. We must get these visas on Saturday. The teachers are coming, and we must get them into the country.

Unfortunately, the visa issue isn't getting fixed. Instead, the stalling and excuse-making continues, along with a lot of avoidance. Harry, accompanied by parents and board members, makes numerous trips to Immigration to pick up the visas, and each time they are denied. Now it is just a couple of days before the teachers are supposed to arrive. Some would soon be in the air. What would happen if they landed at the airport and were then sent back after a trip of more than thirty hours? If they were sent home, not only would it jeopardize the school year; it would seriously damage our ability to recruit American teachers again, partly because these guys would tear us up in the blogosphere.

Finally, I decide I need to take action. I call the official.

He picks up, so I know he's there, but then he hangs up on me. There's no question that Harry is right about this man's intentions. I e-mail Abaarso's supporters and everyone else I can think of and copy the official and my uncle Billeh on all of my communications:

Dear Board of Trustees,
[The official] is blocking visas for the teachers who arrive in 2 days. He has made up every excuse imaginable to avoid giving them to us and now is claiming that he can't unblock them without permission of

the Higher Education Commission. This is of course complete non-sense. If these don't come through and the teachers get stuck in Dubai with no choice but to go home, then all credibility of Abaarso is gone and we will never be able to recruit teachers again.

Early the next morning, I receive a nonchalant e-mail from Billeh:

The matter of the visa is taken care of. The office of the president ordered that the visas be released and that MOE [Ministry of Education] be at airport to meet the teachers.

It turns out Billeh has gotten through to the chief of cabinet, a man named Hersi, who is in China with the president of Somaliland. Hersi, in turn, calls the vice president of Somaliland to have him issue the visas from the presidency. Yet even this order doesn't quite solve the problem.

The day the teachers are due to arrive, Harry and one of our board members, a man named Munir, who runs the local airline, Daallo Airlines, go to see the official at his office in Hargeisa. They are accompanied by our armed guards, protocol for any foreigners in the country who have passed a government checkpoint. The official tries to slip out of his office, telling the men he'll be "right back." Harry has been dealing with his excuses for weeks and there is no time left for more obstruction. He snaps and calls him a liar, causing the official to order our Abaarso guards to place Harry under arrest. "Finally I have you!" he declares, revealing his hand. Munir manages to calm the situation, as the guards stand there frozen, not knowing what to do.

Nobody is arrested, but the tension is making me frantic, as the teachers arriving without visas would be an enormous setback. I stay glued to my computer as the action or the lack thereof continues to unfold. Why is the official putting up such resistance in the visa process? Whatever the reason, it is more than aggravating and annoying, it is outright obstructionist and nearly deals a severe blow to the school. The issue is finally resolved when another official from the Ministry of Education goes to Interior, and the visas are approved and dashed to the airport in time to meet the arriving teachers, who were none the wiser.

While the visa situation is behind us and many of the initial doubters are now on our side, the root cause of our problems remains. I have only seen the tip of my original miscalculation. The question is no longer whether I can create a high-quality school but rather whether I can create such a school in Somaliland. Comparatively, the school part is looking easy.

Fortunately, I was not alone in fighting all of the challenges facing the school. Harry is an exemplary employee; he is like a partner in this start-up. He is willing to throw all of himself into Abaarso, to be creative in his solutions, even to take on personal risk, just like a great entrepreneur. And he isn't the only one, either. There are others like him, and we are about to get great folks in the new class of teachers. Like Harry, they will bring passion and ingenuity to the school, and their day won't stop until the job gets finished. Normally one doesn't find that kind of passion unless there's a profit motive involved, but there is nothing normal about the people who choose to work at Abaarso. Few people are willing to sacrifice so much.

In fact, Abaarso attracts lots of abnormal folks, some of whom I wish it didn't. Some come in an effort to run away from themselves or to look for something that they will most likely not find. Often these people don't stay. Less than halfway through the first school year, we have a teacher decide to leave, well before her one-year contract finished. She is not the only one; teachers who have committed find all kinds of ways not to fulfill their one-year contracts. Many agree to come but don't show up at all. Some come for a short time and then completely disappear. One guy disappeared, reappeared half a year later to once again apply, and then disappeared again (I know, shame on us). Some back out because they have taken other jobs, sometimes admitting it and sometimes not. One who backs out is actually mad at us because she has spent money on coming to Abaarso before changing her mind. One guy takes the job only to say later he's accepted it because he wants to develop a primary school education program. It turns out that he has no interest in the actual job we've hired him for. Some teachers just don't get on the plane or, better yet, get on the first plane but not the second. One teacher goes home before finishing two weeks. Others wait several months before bailing. One comes looking for love and, not finding it, leaves. I don't know how Abaarso could have beaten out any other location as a romantic destination, save maybe Antarctica and the International Space Station.

It is easy to look at these non-success stories critically, and these folks deserve it, but there's also the other side of the coin. The vast majority of teachers are at Abaarso because they want to make the world a better place. They believe in our mission and work tirelessly in a tough place to make it happen. With each of these dropouts, the passionate remaining teachers shine, picking up the slack, so the students won't suffer. Imagine a public school at which the remaining teachers just agree to take on extra work after a colleague leaves. Most teachers don't feel that kind of ownership and many wouldn't even be allowed to do so if they wanted to. But it is different for Abaarso teachers. They aren't doing more because their boss orders it or because they are getting paid extra for the work. They are working harder because that is what Abaarso needs. These teachers are entrepreneurs, and that's what entrepreneurs do.

Our dedicated teachers know that there are some awful people in this world who couldn't care less if they destroy these children's school. For staff like them, Abaarso is not a concept or a school; it is Nimo's and Amal's and Mubarik's school, and we love it as much as we love them. If Abaarso and its students' futures were to be destroyed, then we would never be the same. That is something we cannot let happen.

30

THE HIGHER EDUCATION COMMISSION

The Higher Education Commission is in charge of settling the matter of who will be in charge of Abaarso School: Khadar or me. Had Khadar been a highly capable "Steve Jobs" type, someone who could achieve Abaarso's potential, I would have been happy to step out of the way. Unfortunately, he is nothing of the sort. Abaarso needs a leader who is serious, focused, and hands-on, and Khadar is none of those. If he succeeds in displacing me, and the Higher Education Commission throws me out of the country, I know it will be the end of the school. Many parents feel the same way, which is precisely why they are on our side.

The financial aspects alone should make it an open-and-shut case. I have been the largest donor, the largest lender, the largest fund-raiser, and the funder of last resort every time the school has been in need. Without my financial intervention, the school would have ceased to exist some time ago. No one else, including Khadar, is willing and able to support Abaarso's financial and operational needs, all of which are immediate. Without my backing, the school is insolvent. How absurd it is that I need to fight a war so as to be able to volunteer full-time at the school *and* fund it! Beyond the financial, I have recruited every teacher, overseen every aspect of the school, and managed it from the start. Khadar hasn't slept a single night at the school. Khadar might tell people that this is "Khadar versus Jonathan," but in fact it is "Khadar versus the futures of Nimo, Mohamed, and all of the other kids."

The parents valiantly fight on our side, but the battle is tough. As one government insider tells me, "Things are taking on a clan image," further noting that Khadar has no other defense. This is a very bad turn and not a surprising one if one understands Somaliland. Facts and justice are on our side. Clan is not.

Rumors circulate that the commission has reached a decision: they have switched Khadar's title from "vice chairman" to "chairman" of Abaarso. I learn this is true a few days later, when I am called to the Ministry of Education for a meeting. Once there, I am directed to an office where I am handed a report written in English riddled with typos, grammatical issues, and lines that are either ambiguous or don't have any meaning. I am to follow along on my copy as the report is read to me aloud. I wouldn't have cared about the unprofessional presentation had the content and conclusion not been so disastrous and outright offensive.

In designating Khadar as chairman, the committee has removed Uncle Billeh from that role. Billeh has been chairman from the start, and while the board has not been active, wouldn't the vice chairman also be held responsible for that? They've also given Khadar veto power over any new school board member whom we appoint, a provision I simply cannot accept. He'll stack it with his people and ultimately destroy the school. My tolerance for this whole circus has run out, and at this moment I see that entire room of Higher Education commissioners as my students' executioners. The situation is untenable, and I am fuming.

Still, I hold my tongue as the report continues to be read aloud for my benefit. But when I hear the line where the commission will appoint a Somali deputy managing director to "relieve Jonathan from direct contact with community, workers, and students," I lose it. Of all the items, this is the biggest "fuck you." To me, it is a thinly veiled acceptance of Khadar's lies that I am destroying the culture and can't be trusted, even around the students. I am supposed to head the school, but no longer will I have contact with anyone. That's their position. There is no chance of my accepting these terms, so I have nothing to lose.

"And who do you think will fund this school?" I ask in fury.

The commissioner replies in a self-congratulatory way that he's accounted for that. "We're still letting you lead all the fund-raising."

"Are you really?" I ask. "Oh, that's so generous of you," I continue sarcastically.

I am so angry that I need a few seconds before I launch into my assault. "You have succeeded in handing a great school to your country-man, which he will now destroy, because he has no ability to run it or fund it. You've done this against the will of everyone who should matter, staff, students, parents, management, and funders. I will leave the country, and I will make sure the entire world knows what you've done and that they shouldn't think of investing a dollar in this place. This is why people don't invest more in Africa."

The committee members are stunned.

"We report to a higher authority. This is not finished," one among them says, making clear to the others that there is still room to nego-tiate.

The next move is theirs. They will need to change their report if they want me to accept it. I tell them that there are absolutely no legal grounds to suddenly appoint a new chairman. However, I will compromise on this so long as Khadar actually has to follow a legitimate board that is domi-nated by the students' parents. If they are worried about the reputation of the girls, then they are more than welcome to send a female teacher to live with them. If they want help for me in dealing with the community, then I am sure one of the parents will take that role a couple of days each week. All of that should solve the supposed issues, but I make it clear that there is no chance I will stay in Somaliland without absolute day-to-day control over the operations of the school. We haven't come this far by making Abaarso exactly like every other school in Somaliland. I agree that I will report to the board, and I will follow any legitimate board vote, as that is how a proper organization works. However, that also means that Khadar cannot overstep boundaries anymore.

I walk out of the meeting with the committee seeming to be in agree-ment, and they ask for a letter that states my position. I don't know if they will stick to it, and until I see the next "Final Report," I am not tak-ing any chances.

I call an urgent meeting with the parents to explain what has happened. I tell them that I will not stay in the country under the stated terms. As I put it for them, "Before Khadar had a knife. Now they have given him a gun." To make sure they know I am not bluffing, I tell the parents that school is now closed until I get confirmation that the commission will improve the document with my conditions.

With that, the students start packing up. Everybody is really sad and stunned. I see no other way, as we must make a statement. It works, as the minister of education, a woman named Zamzam, and other members from the Higher Education Commission arrive at the campus. They have heard about me closing the school and want to talk. Joined by a number of parents and students, we gather in our large lecture hall.

Zamzam addresses the students, who are visibly upset, and tries to calm them down. She tells them not to worry, as the adults will take care of the situation. Fadumo raises her hand, stands up, and gives an impassioned speech in English. Rather than make a demand, Fadumo retells a legend that I, too, have heard. "A century ago, the British wanted to establish universities in Somaliland, but it was thought that they'd come as invaders, so our people didn't allow it. Because of our fear, Uganda and Sudan have two of the best universities in Africa that Somali children dream of attending. Are we going to do it again?" Fadumo is a star, standing up for what is right. Someone would later say, "I don't like the way those girls carry themselves," and I know they are referring to Fadumo. "I bet you don't," was all I could think. This world isn't used to strong girls.

When it is my turn to speak, the students stand up for such an ovation that the minister turns to me and says, "They love you. You can't ever leave these kids."

"Then please fix this," I reply.

At the end of the meeting, a student from our charter class approaches me. His name is Guleed. Although he is shy and usually very reluctant to speak in English, he does so now, with tears in his eyes. "I don't understand," he says, his voice heartbreakingly sad and innocent. "I've learned more here than I have ever learned before. Why would someone take that away from me?"

What can I say? Each humanizing moment with the students makes my anger at Khadar extend to everyone who has let this happen. I know that the members of the Higher Education Commission believe they are doing traditional Somaliland compromise, leaving the school but giving Khadar much of what he's asking for, but such a compromise misses the point. It isn't supposed to be a compromise between Khadar and me, because it isn't about us. We are not the ones who need educating. What is "compromised" in appeasing Khadar is the education of children. Not that I can say that this kind of thing isn't happening in the United States. We have compromised our children's education because we don't have the political will to kick out all those responsible for our failed public schools. We are every bit as guilty.

For Abaarso kids, the system was particularly rigged because Khadar abused the fact that the Ministry of Education was led by one of his clansmen. In an American context, the Department of Education favoring someone from a particular region would be extremely improper, but in Somaliland, such positions are actually appointed for the very sake of clan representation. Every subclan expects to get its quota, just like how the American Congress works with its regional representation. While it is possible for the president to remove a minister, doing so unofficially requires making someone else from that subclan a minister in his or her place. This is deemed necessary, as when there is trouble with a subclan, the government sends that subclan's ministers to calm the masses. In fact, it is all but expected that Khadar's subclan should be favored by the Ministry of Education. Not that he left these matters to chance. By all accounts, Khadar had his relatives outside of Somaliland calling the ministry and harassing them about how "they should not be stealing Khadar's school." That put the ministry in a royal mess in which the two job functions—promoting the country's education and representing the subclan—come in direct conflict.

The Higher Education Commission's decision improved Khadar's position, a major issue if my fears about him were correct and he wouldn't be satisfied unless he took over or destroyed the school. In the Higher Education Commission's defense, they failed to understand what the school had already become. As even one supporter would later say, "We thought it was a good school. None of us understood it was this good."

In the end, the Higher Education Commission rewrites the report to reflect that I am the day-to-day manager, that the board will have at least a handful of parents, and that Khadar must follow the directions of the board. While not perfect, the revised report allows me to reopen the school after only a few days.

PART FIVE

TENACITY

It's not that I'm so smart; it's just that I stay with problems longer.

—ALBERT EINSTEIN

31

SELLING SUCCESS

It is September 2012, and one year has passed since the open house at which we announced Mubarik's scholarship to Worcester Academy, and once again parents, students, and dignitaries are filling Abaarso's big hall, eagerly awaiting the next scholarship news. They are about to witness nothing less than a referendum on Mubarik's performance at Worcester Academy—and, in turn, on Abaarso's mission.

I had kept up with Mubarik's progress during infrequent Skype calls with my mother. Mubarik stayed with her during school vacations and holidays, which was a learning experience for both of them. For Mubarik, being in the United States had been a culture shock. He had never seen landscaped lawns, lush forests, extravagant gardens, and so many trees and flowers. He may have been the only person to ever declare Worcester, Massachusetts, to be a place of unparalleled beauty. Upon seeing a landscape crew working on a lawn in Worcester, he remarked something along the lines of, "There's so much grass here, you cut it. Why not use goats?"

Everything had been new for him, even the toilet. The first time I had seen a squat toilet, which is flat with the ground and has no toilet seat, I had absolutely no idea what to do. Mubarik had been no different with a seated toilet. He broke the seat soon after arriving at my mother's house. For my mother, having Mubarik stay with her meant developing a whole new reservoir of patience. To slow the tide of household mishaps, she'd eventually put Post-its on things that needed explanation, like NO METAL on the door of the microwave.

During one of our Skype calls, Mom expressed concern at what she felt was the weight of responsibility I had placed on Mubarik's shoulders. "I know Mubarik feels like the entire future of Abaarso is on his back," she told me.

"Good. I'm glad he was listening," I replied.

"Is that fair?"

"For better or for worse, it is the truth and he needs to treat it that way," I told her. "This is about much more than just Mubarik."

Originally, Worcester Academy hadn't wanted to put Mubarik in an Advanced Placement Calculus class. The teacher, coincidentally one of my old math teachers, felt Mubarik had lots of holes in his knowledge. I agreed with him but asked that he give him a shot anyway, insisting that Mubarik's intelligence and perseverance would help him close the gaps. He'd work overtime to do whatever was necessary.

With the first report card, we got the very good news that our boy could play. He'd caught up in AP Calculus, and the teacher was no longer concerned. AP Chemistry was a struggle, because he'd never done real labs before, but the teacher, a wonderful woman who had previously taught at the college level, adored Mubarik and was patiently working with him. For that matter, all the teachers were patient, especially with him not always being easy to understand. Spoken English had not come quickly to Mubarik, and he still had a lot of trouble with pronunciation.

Worcester Academy isn't a "rich kids'" school per se but, compared to Mubarik's upbringing, even the middle-class students seemed like billionaires. With such a difference in backgrounds, Mubarik could have been isolated and outcast, but he wasn't. Students and faculty embraced him in every possible way. They even had a special day where they added a Somaliland flag to the ceiling of their cafeteria, and they made a Somali meal for the whole school. Their "goat stew" was given Mubarik's Somali stamp of approval.

For his first Thanksgiving, a former Abaarso teacher flew him out to

Santa Clara, California, to spend the holiday. When he got back, Mom took him to Walmart for a few necessities. Standing in line to get a soda, he announced that his "reward had just come in the mail."

"What reward?" she asked.

"The reward from California."

"You got a reward? What did you do?"

"I came in ten," Mubarik said.

"Ten in *what?*"

Mubarik, getting a little frustrated, started to talk louder. People in the line started to take notice. "Ten in the race."

"You were in a race?"

"Yes, Christine entered me in a race and I came in ten."

"Wow," Mom said. "How many runners were there?"

When Mubarik answered "ten thousand," everybody in the Walmart line started clapping. It turned out that he had run in the Silicon Valley Turkey Trot, the largest "Turkey Trot" in the United States.

I wasn't surprised to learn that our former nomad was as good at running without goats as he was with them. Mubarik was fast, and the WA cross-country team had a strong season with Mubarik immediately becoming one of their two star performers. Somalis have a storied history as runners, and in fact, the fastest distance runner in the world is a Somali who competes for the UK. There are endless theories on Somali/ Ethiopian/Kenyan dominance, but it seems to come down to superior long-distance-running genetics. On his first day, Mubarik outran others who'd been training for years.

When the "winter sports" season came, Mubarik decided to wrestle. I was back in the States and visiting WA where I saw the incoming headmaster, a man named Ron Cino, who would succeed Dexter Morse. Cino was a wrestler himself and had just come back from watching Mubarik.

"He's strong and scrappy. He's actually winning his matches," Ron reported.

This was shocking. Mubarik is extremely thin, his chest almost concave, which is perfect for running, not so much for wrestling.

Ron continued. "Of course he didn't get the rules at first and got disqualified from his first bunch of matches." This I could imagine. If Mubarik got in a fight back in Somaliland, there'd be no limitations on things like elbows to the groin.

By the springtime, Mubarik had it all figured out. He was now a competitive track runner, leading WA to their best season in years and catching the attention of coaches at some other schools. He was extremely well liked by both teachers and students. He was earning As and preparing for Advanced Placement exams. On AP exams, students received scores of 1 through 5. A 3 is a passing score and considered to be a solid achievement. Mubarik received a 3 on his AP Chemistry exam, not bad for a kid who eight months earlier had never seen a lab. On AP Calculus, he scored a perfect 5. Our boy most definitely could play.

The future of Abaarso was on Mubarik's back, and he succeeded in carrying the entire school. Ron Cino confirmed that WA was ready to take one of Abaarso's girls for the next year. With that victory we'd at least held serve, but after Mubarik's success at WA, we were in a position to get scholarships for more students. We needed to market his results.

Mom treated Mubarik like family, which meant he was now spending time with my relatives. When my cousin Lisa Weiss met him, she was so impressed that she proceeded to contact her old friend who was now assistant headmaster at Northfield Mount Hermon School, another East Coast prep school. That winter, I went to see its gorgeous, expansive campus in the middle of nowhere in a Massachusetts town near the Vermont border. I visited on a frosty day, armed with Mubarik's transcript. The folks there were interested in the possibility of an Abaarso student, that was for sure, but they weren't interested in someone for just a year. They wanted someone for at least two years, who would eventually graduate from Northfield. *Great*, I thought, *a multiyear deal.* But this set the bar higher. Staying through graduation meant college placement, too, which was a major concern for Northfield. College placement for a full-need, international kid was not going to be easy, and they were not going to be happy if it didn't work out.

Northfield would be one of a number of stops I would make as I began meeting with boarding school administrators and even some college officers about our students. I always had some connection to the places I visited, as I didn't think we'd stand a chance without a personal introduction. A lot of schools would no doubt assume that even the best Somaliland students couldn't make it in their environment, just as Worcester Academy originally had feared. I was only focusing on placing top candidates, the ones who I knew could perform. It seemed we could expand from one scholarship the year before, but I didn't know what was possible. Maybe triple that number?

I saw boarding schools in New England similar to Worcester Academy, as well as others generally considered to be more elite and selective. One of my former business partners, Tom Wieand, even gave me an introduction to Massachusetts Institute of Technology. Tom worked at the MIT endowment, and he put me in touch with MIT's dean of admissions. I met with him and gave him my best sell, even though we were still a year away from our first college applicants. The idea of an Abaarso student at MIT brought chills.

A few months after my visits, the open house at Abaarso to announce our scholarships gets under way with a traditional prayer. One by one I call up the six students who have been awarded scholarships to boarding schools in the States. I tell the audience of students, parents, and dignitaries all about the schools these young people will be attending, as I project photos of the institutions onto a screen. The visuals of the New England boarding schools are absolutely glorious, and everyone oohs and aahs. Deqa is going to Worcester Academy, Mohamed to Northfield Mount Hermon, and Fadumo and Soorer to the Ethel Walker School. Abdikarim (CK) will spend the year at Wilbraham and Monson Academy, and Naima will go to the Taft School. A seventh student, Hamse, has been awarded a scholarship to African Leadership Academy, a high-quality, two-year school in South Africa. ALA is what the British call "college," which is advanced studies prior to attending university. While still young, ALA had already made a global splash, taking top students from across Africa and then sending them on to many of the best universities in the world.

As each student joins me onstage, he or she receives a banner from his new school to hang on the wall of the lecture hall. "In the coming years, let's cover this entire room with banners," I say.

In the second row, I see Edna Adan, whose head is ferociously nodding in agreement. She is the world's most famous Somalilander, renowned for her maternity hospital and her war against female genital mutilation. Edna had been instrumental in my originally coming to Somaliland. She is a friend of Billeh's, and I had met her in New York City in 2006 when I had made a contribution to her hospital in Hargeisa. In her mid-seventies, she is more dynamic and full of life than most people will ever be, which no doubt is how she developed such an impressive résumé. She had been first lady when her husband was prime minister of Somalia; foreign minister of Somaliland from 2003 until 2006; a career nurse in the World Health Organization; and Somaliland's minister of family welfare and social development. Now, here she is at our open house, showcasing her support for Abaarso and displaying her pride for her people.

One of the proudest moments of the day is when Amal takes the stage to congratulate her fellow classmates. I know how difficult this is for her, as she suffers from an intense fear of public speaking. In small groups and one on one, you can't get Amal to shut up, but I've seen her freeze in front of crowds. She has written a heartfelt poem for her friends who are now leaving, and as she begins to read, the fright in her voice melts into sadness. Through tears, she wishes her friends good luck, while highlighting each of their special gifts. She concludes this way:

It's coming sooner than we expected,
Soon we will all be separated,
It's been three years,
And what a journey it has been
A path less traveled by others
But trust me, it was worth it.
This in a way does not mark the end of us,
We started being friends,
And ended up being a family,
And family never ends.

Amal herself is not going to the United States this year, but her brave and thoughtful performance stands in stark contrast to the lives of so many girls in Somaliland. She delivers an impressive send-off and in the process wins over at least one supporter. Somaliland's most famous and strongest woman, Edna Adan, is in tears.

32

NO GOOD DEED GOES
UNPUNISHED

Now that we've accepted the compromise report of the Higher Education Commission, which clarifies the role of Khadar and me, I return to the business of running the school. Although Khadar is difficult to work with, I put in my best effort. However, I am insisting that he and the board take on proper financial planning and accountability rather than just thinking I'll fund every shortfall. Khadar, however, wants my money to come without any real stipulations.

The kids are making incredible progress. To choose our incoming class in our fourth year, we decide to forgo the shared exam with SOS Sheikh and conduct our own. We will write it ourselves and administer it in two locations, Hargeisa and Burao. Because Abaarso is inconvenient for much of the country, it isn't fair that some students should have to drive ten hours to take our exam. Burao is much more centrally located. The people of Burao are excited to learn we will hold an exam in their city. Even the mayor of the city is eager to host us. To ensure the exam goes off without a hitch, we prepare in every way possible. Two months before the test day, Harry goes to the Ministry of Education, where he gets a signed letter giving us permission to hold our test there. We also secure a testing site at a public university in Burao. A few days before the exam, Harry; Mike, our finance manager; Michelle, a teacher; and I travel to Burao to make the final preparations. The country's lack of infrastructure makes it impossible to drive directly from Hargeisa to Burao, so we must first travel three hours northeast to Berbera, and then two hours southeast from there. The only direct road is a brutal drive that will not save any time.

We are going to stay at the home of a Somali doctor who has spent the last forty years in Germany and is now back in Somaliland. We have also arranged for a handful of our students from the Burao area to help register students for the exam—ensuring that there is no cheating is of utmost importance.

In Burao, we spend some of the day visiting local schools and getting potential students excited about coming for the exam. We then go to the university, where we spend several hours arranging the exam room, which requires separating and numbering all of the desks. We have invited the test-taking students to show up to have their pictures and physical measurements taken. This is a precaution to close up a cheating loophole that Harry had discovered at our exam the previous years.

Harry has had lots of testing experience. By this point, he has learned almost all the tricks cheaters use. At our testing site in Hargeisa, he goes from testing room to testing room to monitor the teachers and students and address any issues or requests that might arise. One year, when he stepped outside to buy some soft drinks for our proctors, he recognized one of our male students sitting in the driver's seat of a parked car. This struck him as odd, so he walked over to see what was going on. In the backseat was another of our male students, as well as a boy he didn't know, who was introduced to him as a relative of the other two. When he asked what they were doing there, they told him they were waiting on a friend who was inside taking the exam.

Harry didn't think anything of it until several days later when he saw this same young man, the supposed "relative," reporting to Abaarso School as one of our incoming ninth graders. Harry then realized that he had used a substitute to take the exam for him the day that Harry had seen him in the car. Of course, we could not let the boy enroll at our school under those circumstances. Future checks revealed that many times, potential students were sending substitutes to take the exam for them. To prevent this, we started announcing in Somali that we were checking all names and photos, and anyone found taking the exam for someone else would be brought to the police. I remember one guy who dashed full-speed out of the room and compound after the announcement. Now we photograph and measure all of our test takers prior to the exam to quash this kind of fraud. The same face who registers needs to belong to the one who takes the test *and* the one who shows up at the school on registration day.

In Burao, my teachers, our volunteer students, and I spend much of the afternoon feverishly working to get the exam room ready, registering our potential test takers, and setting out test books for the following day. To curb the cheating, we have printed up hundreds of test books with different orders of questions and answers so students sitting near each other cannot copy off another's paper. After hours of setup, we are finally ready. Locking the doors behind us, we head to dinner, charged up for the coming day.

The following morning, we arrive at the university to see hundreds of kids waiting outside to take the test. But we quickly learn there is a problem. The grounds people are telling us that the Ministry of Education has not sanctioned us, and we aren't going to be allowed to administer our exam. Soon, soldiers armed with AK-47s arrive and tell us the same thing. I start calling all of the local people I can think of who support Abaarso to show up and help us. Well-connected and respected people begin to come to our aid.

We try to get in touch with contacts at the Ministry of Education, but we can't reach anyone. We hear that there is a government official in town, and we arrange to have him and others, including Harry, meet at the mayor's office in Burao to figure out a solution. The mayor wants the test to proceed as planned, but he is in a quandary, as he seems to be receiving contradictory orders. Harry goes to the meeting; I stay behind at the university with the teachers and students. Harry proceeds to tell those in attendance at the meeting our side of the story, hoping to convince them that what is happening is unfair. He explains that we are trying to give the people of Burao and eastern Somaliland access to our school; hundreds clearly want it, but someone is obviously blocking us.

The government official and the mayor tell Harry to give them five minutes to talk, but when ten minutes pass and they have not returned,

Harry grows unsettled. Finally, the mayor reenters the room, where the others in attendance begin speaking to each other in Somali. Harry does not have a translator and cannot understand what is being said. Finally, he stands up and looks outside the office, hoping to see the government official on his way into the room. Instead, he finds the hallway empty. He searches the area but can't find him, so he asks a watchman by the front gate if he has seen anyone leave the premises. He learns that the official just left in his car, so he reports this to the mayor. When the mayor reaches the official on the phone, he finds the gentleman well on his way back to Hargeisa. We will receive no help from him.

Deflated, we all return to the doctor's house to regroup and figure out what to do. The government thinks we are at a hotel, and we learn that someone has sent police to search the hotels so they can arrest us and send us back to Hargeisa. Eventually, we report to the police ourselves, and they tell us we must get out of town. We comply and make the long journey back, our car filling with dust every time we slow down, because on top of everything else, the back windshield accidentally shattered when we closed the trunk that day.

Back in Hargeisa, the U.S. embassy in Djibouti has heard about the situation and calls to check on our safety. Although this is reassuring, I know they can't do much about it. We stop at a restaurant to eat and discuss the situation. Why did this blockage of our test happen? Was it Khadar using his clan connections in the government to disrupt Abaarso's recruitment efforts and make us look like outlaws? Was it the director of the exam board seeking revenge against us for not giving him more respect? Was it someone at SOS Sheikh, thinking we were trying to steal the brightest students from the Burao pool? Or someone from the for-profit Burao schools angry that we were taking their students?

That evening, we learn that someone from the Ministry of Education has gone on television to explain how we tried to break the law by administering the entrance exam without permission. Right or wrong, I'm now convinced that we will not receive any justice in this country.

I make the decision to go to war with the ministry, too. I felt wronged by them, and I couldn't tell if they and Khadar were joined together against us anyway. I give a group of reporters the official letter, signed by the Ministry of Education, approving the administration of our exam, and they publish it the following day, along with our side of the story. Only later will I realize that embarrassing the government has probably been a strategic mistake. My moral outrage at the injustice had allowed me to tell myself otherwise.

I call a consultant at the Ministry of Education and tell him he knows we are right, and it is his responsibility to fight for a just outcome. When I run into him a week later, he is furious at me for "blackmailing his conscience." That one line sums up my view of what is being done to Abaarso. They know we are right, they aren't going to do anything to help, and they are actually angry with me for pointing out their moral obligation. My head rings with the Einstein quote often repeated by Fahima, a favorite student of mine: "The world will not be destroyed by those who do evil, but by those who watch them without doing anything."

After the Burao exam disaster, I decide I will look at moving Abaarso to Dire Dawa, Ethiopia, where Somalis also live and are welcome. This is a crazy idea, to start from scratch in a new country, one that doesn't even allow free speech, and to invest my heart and soul in a new place. But it is the only way I see of getting away from a seemingly unwinnable situation, in which everything we've created will ultimately be given to a man who has neither the ability nor the desire to sustain it. It seems that in Somaliland neither contracts nor letters of permission matter. There seems to be no rule of law here other than Khadar getting to call the shots on his clan's land, even without the support of the people who live there. I can't keep on building something if the country is going to let him knock it down.

We keep the school open and continue to run it for those students currently enrolled. Despite Mubarik's success at Worcester Academy and several other students following him to the United States, we do not take a new ninth-grade class of students for the fall of 2012. This is a decision that will affect the lives of the many young people who hope that admittance to Abaarso will change the course of their lives. Many see Abaarso as their only option, the only escape route. I later hear one story in particular from a student whose childhood friends had taken the Abaarso entrance exam the year before but had not scored well enough to gain admittance. The two boys had studied hard in preparation to try again this year. Upon learning that Abaarso will not be taking an incoming class, the two young men saw no other option but to leave Somaliland. They boarded boats for Yemen, hoping to eventually reach Europe. One died during the crossing; the other became stuck at a refugee camp in Italy, where he still remains, unable to secure the paperwork necessary to leave the camp. Stories like this are heartbreaking. But how can we take on more students, promising them an education, when it seems their country will not allow us to fulfill that promise?

33

A SOMALI AMONG THE ELITE

It is early November 2012, in Windsor, Connecticut, and it is a gorgeous day for runners, around fifty degrees and sunny, although somewhat on the breezy side. Today, fifteen of the top prep schools in New England, including Andover, Exeter, and Choate, are brought together for the Division I Cross Country Championship, sponsored by the New England Preparatory School Track Association. This is America's elite, with those three schools alone boasting presidents and senators, from Franklin Pierce and Daniel Webster to John F. Kennedy, George H. W. Bush, and George W. Bush, as alumni.

The scene summons all of the clichés associated with prep-school America. Every prep school has a large tent, each labeled with its easily identifiable logo, where the athletes can stretch and complete their pre-race preparations. Several hundred friends and family members have already parked their SUVs and BMWs, and are gathered in a football field–sized area around the starting line. Decked out in the apparel of whatever school they are rooting for, they soak in the atmosphere and thrive in the pre-competition passion that energizes these kinds of events. It surely seems to be a place where a slight young Somali might be out of his comfort zone.

If you've ever watched a cross-country meet, you know that the spectator experience is different from the spectator experience at most sporting events. You are not in a seat or confined to one location. At the beginning, you see a mass of runners in their first few hundred yards, but when they disappear around a turn or into a wooded area, you move, too, hustling to another viewing spot where the runners will pass by a short time later.

By this second viewing, the runners are sorting into groups. You see a lead pack of a dozen or so, some who are top runners, others who are temporarily pushing the pace, then a second pack, then the runners start to string out. Today, it is easy to spot Mohamed, and not only because the vast majority of runners are white. Most of the runners also have a different physique, quite tall and muscular. At five foot six and about 125 pounds, "Mo," as he is endearingly known, looks like a boy among men. But he isn't running like he doesn't belong. He is up with the leaders in the first group, running smoothly and easily.

Four months earlier, Mohamed had seen his first escalator at the airport in Addis Ababa. He had not even understood that once he stepped on, the escalator would break into stairs. He had placed his suitcase behind him along the separation between steps, and the luggage hit a very unfortunate traveler twenty feet below him when the moving stairs caused it to fall backward.

If the modern world hadn't shocked Mohamed enough, the lavishness of the facilities at Northfield Mount Hermon must have exceeded anything this tribal chief's son could have imagined. The day I had dropped him off, he had been silent, leaving me hoping he was just trying to take it all in.

When Metta Dael, the admissions officer at NMH, told me they were accepting Mohamed, she immediately wanted to know if they'd been snookered, with our best students going elsewhere. "Don't worry," I said, "we have a few top students with different qualities, but Mohamed is as good as any we've got."

Metta's question probably highlighted NMH's sensitivity to its reputation, which was excellent but not historically in the same league as Andover, Exeter, and St. Paul's School. That is unfortunate, as from my perspective, it is an exceptional school, balancing rigor with a welcoming, nurturing environment. It is where I'd look first to send my own children. Before Mohamed even arrived in the States, he received a visit from an NMH ambassador. The school paid for Grant Gonzalez, the head of the NMH boys' cross-country team, to visit Abaarso School. A young and energetic teacher, Grant had seen Mubarik run for Worcester Academy at a track meet between the two schools and was so impressed that he contacted me to arrange a summer visit to Abaarso. For Mohamed, Grant's visit put a friendly face on a daunting situation. For Abaarso, Grant's visit opened students' eyes to the reality of these opportunities at American boarding schools.

Prior to Grant's arrival, Mohamed had done a half marathon for fun, hadn't trained, and finished in the top 20. That's not how things work for most people, and it also wasn't typical Mohamed. When he did something, he did it with extreme focus and dedication, but while that race convinced him that he had potential, he saw no future in running. He had no coach, no running gear, and no training facility. Grant changed that.

Varsity cross-country is Mohamed's first time participating in an organized sport. He has told me how safe and peaceful he feels when he is running, but I think it is more than that. Cross-country and track require the ultimate in discipline, with the rigorous training schedule, the mindful self-pacing, and the careful diet. To me, Mohamed is the human embodiment of discipline.

At Northfield Mount Hermon, Mohamed is one of only twelve varsity runners. Grant has told me that his top runner, Henry Colt, has taken Mohamed under his wing. Grant used to think that Mohamed might be able to fill the number two spot behind Henry, even in his first year. But the first handful of races have corrected his prediction. Mohamed is already NMH's top runner.

At today's meet, the next viewing opportunity is right about the midpoint of the race. The front-runners appear, and Mo is still right there, running steadily in tenth place. "Go, Mo! Go, Mo!" we yell. This would be a fantastic finish if he could just hold on to it. Top 10 in his first championship race. We'll know in seven minutes. My uncle Eli, my mother's brother, asks me what result would disappoint me now. I say, "Are you kidding? We are watching Mohamed run for the New England Championships. This is all the house's money."

Mohamed isn't the only Abaarso student striving to make his mark in America. Deqa, now a full-time Worcester Academy student, is firing on all cylinders. While physically Deqa is as slow as Mohamed is fast, Worcester Academy has introduced her to a host of new opportunities, and she is doing the equivalent of running for the championship. At her first Model United Nations, an event held at Boston College, she won Top Delegate. She also entered Worcester Academy's Dexter Prize Contest, which is a public speaking challenge performed in front of the entire school. I remembered this competition well from my time at WA and told Deqa to be very careful; the same students compete year after year and spend months rehearsing for their speeches. She didn't heed my words, instead memorizing the speech the night before. Deqa was so good that it didn't matter that she had fallen asleep before finishing her preparation. She made up a different ending and apparently pulled it off so well that she won First Prize. When I asked around if any other foreign student had ever taken this prize, no one at Worcester Academy could remember a foreign student winning. Deqa had done it in her third language.

Fadumo, too, is rising to the challenges at her prep school. Her visa difficulties solved, she is adjusting to life at Ethel Walker, on all-girls' school in Simsbury, Connecticut. She isn't competing for championships, but she is fighting her own war. She has been shortchanged by the chemistry class at Abaarso, and I am realizing it only now. Our chemistry teacher had been dealing with personal struggles that were impacting the classroom, which I hadn't noticed. The problem was compounded when the teacher left midterm. We tried to replace him with two different teachers from Hargeisa, but both were disasters. Teaching in Hargeisa involves educators bouncing between several schools each day, racking up credit hours and pay, with quality and preparation suffering in return. When these educators briefly came to Abaarso, our students, who know good teaching from bad, quickly picked up on it. "That's a stupid question, so I'm not going to answer it," one would tell a student in response to a question she posed.

As a result, our top students in the States—Deqa, Mohamed, and Fadumo—are nowhere near ready for the AP Chemistry expected of them. They hadn't had the necessary instruction and had never seen a proper lab. Participating in AP Chemistry would be like learning the basic chemistry and the advanced chemistry at the same time: maybe not impossible, but not a mountain students should be expected to climb. I tell the three to drop AP and take regular chemistry instead.

Fadumo's schedule is plenty challenging even without this AP course. She is also homesick, missing her huge family across the world. I have gone to see her a few times because I am worried; but despite being down, she is a real fighter. I see a lot of my sister, Beth, in her: both under five feet tall, both talents, both sometimes falling down, but always getting back up and seeing the challenge through to an admirable completion. Fadumo can't swim, but she still insists on joining an outdoor group for a rope swing into a river (with a life jacket). She's never been in a play or even seen one, but she tries out and gets a real part. Naturally, Fadumo refuses to drop AP Chemistry.

Slowly, Fadumo begins to see Ethel Walker as a second home. She makes new friends, perhaps having now accepted that to do so was in no way a slight of her old ones in Somaliland. By year's end, she takes the exams for AP Chemistry and AP Calculus, scoring impressive 4s on both.

Soorer, a girl from our second class, is also thriving at Ethel Walker, performing well in her classes and playing every sport she can. Soorer is the one who keeps the Abaarso students abroad connected, lifting their spirits if they are feeling low or lonely.

Abdikarim—better known as CK—is bringing a new perspective to his classmates at Wilbraham and Monson Academy in Wilbraham, Massachusetts. When the school has an "international day" with each student holding his country's flag, CK proudly waves his Somaliland colors for all to see. When there is a bake sale, where most students typically stand behind their table of sweets to sell the goods, CK prefers taking a batch around the room, outselling everyone else. He has exactly the type of personality that Wilbraham and Monson's headmaster likes. The student body is learning just by being around him. CK is named a proctor, and the headmaster commits to helping him get into college.

Naima is embracing all there is to offer at the Taft School in Watertown, Connecticut. In terms of academic and even social rigor, Taft is about as serious as you can get, no doubt eclipsing a good number of colleges. Taft's admissions director had asked for a spirited all-around student, and we suggested Naima for the part. Naima is gregarious and fun-loving, and within days of arrival at Taft is trying out for every activity. But Taft's competitiveness soon takes a toll on her. She is not finding it easy and, worried about her, I go to see how she is doing.

I cautiously ask Taft's headmaster what he thinks of her performance. "She's going to make it!" he exclaims, showing both excitement and surprise. "We had our review of every student in the school, and Naima is absolutely competing here." Behind his words is a reality that he reiterates for me. Taft is ranked as one of the top schools in all of the United States. Naima is going to *make it* there, and that she can is in itself an amazing feat worth celebrating. Like the result of Mohamed's race, the success of all these students means that, in the parlance of Las Vegas, we are playing with the house's money.

Adjusting to life in the United States hasn't come easily. As one student said, "The United States is not a different country, it's a different planet." To help the students' transition, my mom and her friends have spent weeks preparing extra special care packages for them. Each student receives sheet sets with matching comforters that will help them fit into the elite boarding school scene. Not only do Mom and her friends purchase nice room decor, but they have also studied the trending dress codes and buy or collect ski jackets and backpacks that will be in style.

Once the kids are settled in at their various schools, Mom, her friends, and her two brothers, Eli and Bill, act as their surrogate parents. They go to parent-teacher conferences, musical and theater performances, track races and soccer games. During school holidays, the students stay with Mom in Worcester, even addressing her as "Mum" or "Mum Susan." She manages to get them free gym memberships and refurbished bicycles and makes sure they have appropriate movies to watch.

The learning curve in these early years is steep. Over Thanksgiving 2012, Mom is impressed at how neatly Mohamed is making his bed. It doesn't even look slept in. In fact, it is not slept in. He is sleeping on top of the quilt, probably freezing. It turns out that we need to tell all the kids to sleep under the sheets, top sheets being uncommon in Somaliland.

Hosting these young guests proves challenging for Mom. She is a self-described clean freak, and with all these teenagers in the house, clean is impossible. Students pull the drain out of the bathtub, break the seat off the toilet, unfurl the decorative Roman shades, turn off the oil burner, melt plastic in the oven, leave wet towels everywhere. Mom loves them all and knows they don't mean to do damage, but keeping everything functioning is getting away from her.

To alleviate some of the pressure on Mom, she and I start contacting Somali families living in the New England area to see if they are interested in hosting students. Some have been here for many years and are very Americanized. Others are more traditional. Many families are thrilled with the idea and want to be involved, and soon we have wonderful Somali families all over the East Coast hosting students for weeks and months at a time. Still, some seem baffled about why we are doing all of this for the students, but they, too, love these young people and want to play their part in these kids' success stories. They provide a touch of Somaliland my mom cannot, frying traditional meat pies, celebrating Muslim holidays, and immersing these adolescents in the sights and smells closer to their traditional home.

Our family friends have also been a great support for the students. They drive them to the train, invite them to dinner, and collect winter jackets and quilts for them. Mom's friend Jill, a clothier by profession, is the go-to person for advice on prom gowns and graduation dresses. Several friends who have been "matched" with a student early on have developed strong mentor relationships that are just as important as their financial support. Thank heavens for the help.

Abaarso students are not free of the typical adolescent angst. They are homesick as well as anxious to make us proud. That struggle can take its toll on students' self-confidence and lead to not-so-unusual adolescent depression. Mom visits whoever is suffering, offers encouragement, and even gets students into counseling if the situation warrants it.

What does it take for students to be happy and successful in boarding schools or colleges? Academic strength and perseverance are key. But the students also need to feel they belong, and they need to know how to negotiate the system. Most middle-class kids I know just assume that they will succeed in college and that their parents are behind them to offer whatever help they need. They are taught how to seek out faculty, use the college's support system, advocate for themselves, and call home when they have questions. While all that hovering can also be a problem, it gives them a sense of safety. On the other hand, kids from underserved communities often do not learn to seek help and may not have someone to offer sound advice that comes from experience. Even American students who are the first in their families ever to go to college report feeling like a phony, wondering when someone will realize they are impostors. We will not allow this to happen to our Abaarso kids in the United States. They are foreigners, but we cannot allow them to feel like they don't belong.

So why did my mother volunteer for this job as "surrogate mother" to my students? She had grown up in the 1950s, reading *Little Women*, *Five Little Peppers and How They Grew*, stories of children who overcame hardships. By far her favorite was *Little Men*, in which one of the characters, Jo March, runs a school for needy boys. Mom says I have given her the role of a lifetime—the chance to be Jo.

In a way, Mohamed has given *me* the chance of a lifetime, the chance to cheer on an athlete and scholar who has proven that Abaarso can compete with the best. Eli and I are jockeying for space at the finish line at the cross-country championships, where everyone is waiting for the leaders to show themselves. They will soon pop out of the woods about a hundred yards away. It doesn't surprise us at all to see a tall, blond, longstriding youth in an Exeter shirt come into sight ahead of the rest. Exeter is the defending champion and is the favorite to win again.

The next runner to emerge represents Belmont Hill School, but right behind him comes the unexpected and unmistakable diminutive figure of Mohamed. Yes, Mohamed Hussein, the Somali from Abaarso School, with less than six months of training and coaching under his belt, has taken third place in the New England Prep School Cross Country Championships, just sixteen seconds behind the champion.

Any other kid would be over the moon after such a performance. Mohamed isn't dissatisfied, but he also makes no distinction between the house's money and his own. He's had a taste, and he wants more. He tells Eli, "If I keep improving, I can win it next year."

The runner from Belmont Hill School will go on to be a multisport star at Harvard, so Mo is traveling in distinguished company. But Mo is no slouch. He leads Northfield to its highest finish in years and demonstrates that he is poised to challenge the world's elite. And, like the other top finishers, Mohamed is proving no less capable in the classroom. He's becoming a star in every way.

In his senior year, Mohamed proves almost impossible to beat. In his penultimate race, he'd give NMH back their course record by beating the time of an Exeter student who'd previously been the fastest. Then, at the New England Championship, hosted by the prestigious 150-year-old St. Paul's School in Concord, New Hampshire, John Kerry's old stomping grounds, Mo is ready. He wins the event while breaking a decade-old course record.

For his efforts, Mohamed is named Gatorade Massachusetts Boys' Cross Country Runner of the Year. In the world of elite New England preparatory schools, Mohamed Hussein has put Somaliland and Abaarso on the map.

34

TWENTY-SEVEN SCHOOLS IN
TWENTY-FIVE DAYS

My fears for the future of Abaarso make me all the more determined to promote my current Abaarso students to American universities. My uncle Eli has agreed to help me. He is driving the rental car we are using for our swing through the Midwest, and I'm in the passenger seat, thinking as I watch the scenery go by. We are going to visit as many schools as we can in three weeks.

I am like a traveling salesman, only my product is back in Somaliland, and it is the Abaarso students. For the last few years, I've championed them to anyone who will listen: Somalis, potential teachers, and donors. But my first class is now in its senior year, so the futures of those students are my complete focus. Abaarso being a great school isn't enough. For them to reach their potential, they'll need more education than Abaarso can provide.

We head south on Interstate 35 in Minnesota, coming upon the Iowa border, where we'll stay the night in a Comfort Inn near Ames. Today has been long. We left Minneapolis early, visiting Carleton College by late morning, and then St. Olaf College by late afternoon. While I am in the meetings, Eli relaxes and hangs around, which is one reason he does 75 percent of the driving. He also likes it.

After dinner and some sleep, we grab a quick breakfast at the motel's buffet. I get online and communicate with Harry and others back at Abaarso, making sure everything is okay.

Looking at the day ahead, we'll continue south on I-35, then drive east on Interstate 80 to Grinnell College. From there we turn around and head west to Des Moines, then south to Kansas City where we'll stay the night. It will be the first of three consecutive five-hour driving days, not that the other days are light ones. These Midwest roads are flat and straight, which if nothing else makes for simple directions. As Eli says, to get to Kansas City from Grinnell we just drive to Des Moines and take a left.

The town of Grinnell is not a beauty, nor is it a destination unless you are going to Grinnell College. But the campus is lovely, as I'd expect from a highly rated and wealthy private liberal arts college. Eli drops me off at admissions, which is not the normal converted residence usually found. Instead, it is a large two-story glass building that seems like it holds more than an admissions office.

By this point, I can already make a coffee-table book titled *Admissions Offices of America*, with photos as well as rankings on view, friendliness, and snacks, with points off for those without easy parking.

I have little time to sample Grinnell's offering before the international admissions director, Jon Edwards, comes to get me. I've never met him before, but he is the reason for today's long drive.

Edwards is friendly and easy to talk to. He seems genuinely pleased that I've come all the way to Iowa to see him. Not that the school doesn't get visits from college counselors and consultants, but Grinnell isn't like an East Coast school that you can easily string together with five other colleges in a close time frame. Besides, I am not a college counselor. I am the founder of a school, and that is a novelty, if nothing else.

Grinnell is a top-20-ranked liberal arts college, but not everyone knows of it. This is true of many small liberal arts colleges. Even Williams College and Amherst College, generally ranked number 1 and number 2 among private liberal arts colleges, lack the brand recognition of the big universities whose football teams play nationally on Saturday afternoons. But University of Iowa, an hour east, and Iowa State University, back in Ames where we slept, are not possible destinations for Abaarso students. It is not that they are more selective than Grinnell, because the opposite is true, and by a wide margin. Grinnell's acceptance rate is under

30 percent, while those well-known state schools accept around 80 percent of applicants.

The difference is money. Few universities fund international students, and even fewer provide full funding. The ones that do provide full funding almost always limit those spots, and they absolutely take funding needs into consideration when deciding whether or not to admit someone. Those colleges that are truly "need-blind" for international students can be counted on one hand, and they have names like Harvard, Yale, and Princeton. Those are the schools not worried about their own funding, but they are also the most elite in the world.

The state universities are rightfully most concerned about funding students in their state. Visiting them would most likely be a 100 percent waste of everyone's time, so my trip is focused on the high-potential colleges, places like Grinnell that are excellent schools, not as competitive for entry as Harvard, Yale, and Princeton, but still with the money to fund our full-need international students.

Grinnell is actually one of the richest colleges in America, especially in proportion to its small student body. Its endowment is more than double Iowa State University's, and 50 percent more than the University of Iowa's, yet its student population is only 5 percent of those massive schools. They have a lot more money to spend on far fewer students. And to their credit, they don't sit on their pot of gold. They are known to be very generous with financial aid.

The primary purpose of my meeting here is not as much to get to know Grinnell as it is for Grinnell to get to know Abaarso. Still, it is important to listen to what the school has to say, because we need to make sure we are sending them the applicants who fit what they are looking for and who will excel here.

I have now done dozens of these meetings and have matured from my early days when I thought that I was begging for a favor. While I am asking the colleges to commit massive sums of money, in Grinnell's case $240,000 per student over four years, the relationship is more symbiotic than one might think. I have something special to offer. I have children from a place where these schools haven't received applicants in decades. And to people like Jon Edwards, diversity is not about checking boxes, it is about the educational benefits that come from people of varying backgrounds living together. My students are mostly from a breakaway unrecognized country within the world's number 1 failed state, Somalia. They are Muslims, they have grown up in a clan society, and some even grew up nomadic. These students aren't boxes; they are perspectives that Grinnell wants in its classrooms.

Grinnell has the ability and desire to fund and build a student body that represents world diversity. The issue on Mr. Edwards's mind is whether our students can do the work at Grinnell—a fair question and one I am definitely used to, all the way back to my meeting with Dexter Morse at Worcester Academy. Fortunately, I haven't come unarmed, and I break out my evidence—Mubarik's performance at Worcester Academy. Sure, he is only one student and, no, he isn't yet in college, but he has excelled, even in Advanced Placement classes. From there, I tell Mr. Edwards about other students now in the United States and what I know of their academic performance. My message: don't worry, our kids can compete.

At meeting's end, I get a tour of the campus. It is a one-on-one with a nice young man who is a Grinnell student. I am glad for this opportunity, because it is a good way to learn about the school. While we take the traditional tour, I try not to let it distract our conversation, because the buildings are unimportant to me. Of course, they have state-of-the-art facilities; Grinnell College has a $1.7 billion endowment. I'm not worried about the dorm rooms being too small, since our students are currently jammed into our rooms; and I'm not worried about the quality of the food, which has to be an upgrade from our Abaarso cuisine. No, my two big questions about Grinnell are whether it will be too liberal for some of my students, and if there will be enough here for those looking to get an education geared toward careers in business or engineering. It is about finding the right fit.

"So how was it?" Eli asks me as we drive away from campus and merge onto I-80 West.

"It went well. I liked the international admissions director."

"You think they'll take someone?"

"Eventually, yes."

"Not this year?"

"I just don't know which school is going to be the first to give us a chance," I say.

We are working in a world where the decision makers aren't necessarily incentivized to take chances. From what I'm told, when a student fails, professors are known to say, "Obviously that kid wasn't going to hack it here," then point to whatever weaknesses exist in his or her application. They aren't known to come in and congratulate admissions directors and officers on a job well done.

"I don't think they are overly worried about the SATs," I add. "They get that it isn't the end-all, be-all."

SATs are always a conversation in meetings. The problem is not the SAT itself, which legitimately does measure some current abilities, but rather how many schools interpret the scores. To many colleges, a 550 is better than a 500, a 600 better than a 550, and that's the end of the story. In some respects this is, of course, true, but it must be remembered that the SAT score is not an end in itself. Its purpose is to predict who will succeed at a given college.

As an example of the SAT's limitations, let's assume that an Abaarso student takes the SAT in his fourth year and gets a 530 reading score. That is the 58th percentile, meaning he has scored higher than 58 percent of "College-Bound Seniors," which has already eliminated all those students who don't even bother to take the SAT. Let's compare him to a privately schooled student in New York City who also takes the SAT in his twelfth-grade year, but for him that is his thirteenth year of excellent private schooling. In second grade, this student had superior English to what the Abaarso student had in ninth grade. The New York kid gets a 600 reading score, which is the 79th percentile.

Yes, at the time of the exam, the New Yorker's vocabulary and reading are better than that Abaarso student's. This the SAT correctly measures. But will he be a better student in college? If I'm an admissions officer comparing these two cases with the given information, it is a no-brainer to take the student new to English and new to proper education who somehow still beat 58 percent of college-bound seniors. Any student from that background who reaches over a 500 in such a short period of time has accomplished something miraculous and is growing by leaps and bounds every day. The available evidence shows a student who puts tremendous effort into his studies. By comparison, what percentile do you think the English-speaking New Yorker would have gotten if he had three years to prepare for the Japanese national exam? If he got to the 50th percentile, I'd be pretty darn impressed and think that the kid is a force to be reckoned with.

The SAT makes no adjustment for background, rate of improvement, or a student's work ethic, all of which are highly relevant to a student's chance of success. My student with the 530 reading score is improving so quickly that he'd probably be over 600 if tested again a year later. The test is also tightly timed, and it is this time factor that costs our students so many points. They can't read and answer all the questions in the twenty-five minutes allotted. In Nimo's third year at Abaarso, I gave her an SAT reading section and told her not to worry about time. She took thirty-two minutes instead of twenty-five, and she got all but one reading question right. On the actual test, that seven minutes would be devastating to her score.

I was once at a table of admissions officers that included a representative from a well-known New England liberal arts college. She boasted, "If you don't get a 600 reading score, then you can't make it at [my school]." What a load of nonsense. Emory is at least as reputable as her college, so I know full well what is needed to "make it" at her school. In college, each week students have about fifteen hours of classes, which averages about two hours per day. Even if they sleep eight hours per night, that leaves fourteen hours a day free, not exactly the tightly timed environment of the SAT. Nimo would have that extra seven minutes to do her reading. If she didn't know a word, she could look it up. If she wasn't sure on a writing issue, she could go to the writing center.

Mostly, college is about focus, work ethic, and making the most out of available resources. It is about being tenacious, not stopping until the job is done right, and prioritizing studying over partying. An admissions director once told me that when his prominent university analyzed their dropout pool, they found it consisted disproportionately of high SAT scorers who were high school underperformers. In all probability, the dropouts were the kids who came from good backgrounds, had solid fundamentals, but weren't disciplined.

That prominent university is the only one I know of that does a thorough analysis comparing the various inputs, such as the SAT and students' backgrounds, to students' primary output, performance in college. It is the same analysis we do at Abaarso so that we can make our admissions decisions best match with actual performance. One would think every admissions officer would be constantly referencing her internal manual about what predicts success in her college. One would be wrong. That's why instead some say idiotic things like "If you don't get a 600 reading score, then you can't make it at my school."

Eli and I pull into a Kansas City motel where we will stay the night. Tomorrow we will drive south to the small town of Nevada, Missouri, home to little-known Cottey College, a mostly two-year institution that's women only. I've heard about Cottey from the admissions director at Smith College, who speaks very highly of it. I need as many leads as I can get.

Our visit to Cottey isn't the end of our day. From there, we drive across Missouri until we reach St. Louis. I am meeting with the admissions director at Washington University the following day, and there is no time to waste there, either, as we are going to spend that night in Kentucky.

By our second week, Eli and I have seen Oberlin, Culver Military Academy, St. Mary's College, University of Chicago, Northwestern, Carleton, St. Olaf, and Grinnell. In addition to Cottey and Washington University, we still have Kentucky's Berea College, Ohio Wesleyan University, Kenyon College, Dennison University, Dickinson College, Gettysburg College, Mercersburg Academy, Franklin and Marshall College, Muhlenberg College, Lafayette College, and Lehigh University. We then drive back to Eli's house in Connecticut, and from there I go to my mother's in Worcester late in the evening on October 26. For me this trip had started even before I'd met up with Eli in Pittsburgh. It had begun in Connecticut on October 2, when I'd met with admissions people from Choate Rosemary Hall, Wesleyan University, Miss Porter's School, Yale University, Taft, and Loomis Chafee School, before flying to D.C. and then driving with a friend to Pittsburgh. In total, I will have seen twenty-seven schools in twenty-five days and driven much farther than the length of the United States. And even that great distance does not come close to describing how many schools I have visited before and those I will see after those three weeks in October.

I am planting lots of seeds, and at least one has to take. Our students and our school desperately need at least one of these colleges to let us show what we can do.

35

SAT TRIP

Back in January 2010, I had requested that the College Board recognize Abaarso as an official testing center for the SAT. The College Board had once listed Somalia as having one official test center, but this site had been closed years ago because of a U.S. embargo on commerce and trade with Somalia. We needed to establish a test center in Somaliland because anything short of that would put our students at a tremendous disadvantage. Without Abaarso being a test center, the only alternative for our students would be a multiday bus trip to Addis Ababa in Ethiopia, to sit for the exam there. Our first class of students would be ready to take the SAT in October 2012, so I wanted to have everything in place well before then.

My first correspondence with the College Board went unanswered, so I e-mailed several more times, each time receiving a computer-generated response with no follow-up from anyone. This changed in March 2011 when a freelance journalist by the name of Patrick Adams asked the College Board about the situation. Remarkably, that same day, a response was forthcoming. The e-mail read:

> We wish to reach out to Mr. Jonathan Starr immediately to
> establish a center convenient for his students. Students in Africa

should never, ever need to cross a national border to take the SAT, nor travel 18 hours by bus.

Heartened by this response, I immediately forwarded an application to establish a test site here at Abaarso. When two more months passed without a word, we wrote to check on its status.

I cannot stress how important it is to move this process forward. Our students are the brightest and hardest working in Somaliland, and we are working to prepare them for the SAT. Allowing us to move forward in the application process to be ready in September 2012 is critical. Please let me know if there have been any developments on your end.

But no further communications were forthcoming, and by early summer the College Board stopped responding to our requests for updates. In November, one of our teachers, Abel McDonnell, had completed his assignment with Abaarso and was back in the States. He had been working on the SAT test-center issue while in Somaliland and offered to facilitate the process by going to the organization's New York office to meet with someone in person. Abel's requests for a face-to-face went unanswered, but on November 23, we received an e-mail from a program associate at the College Board, inquiring as to whether our school, or, more generally, our area of Hargeisa, used or had access to any shipping services such as DHL or UPS. We were told that serving as an SAT test center would require international shipments, and the College Board was interested in determining our available shipping options. While this seemed promising, ultimately our application was rejected in March 2012 because of the "issue of security shipping SAT tests and materials directly to your school," as "security issues are too challenging at this time."

Because of U.S. sanctions and embargoes on business and trade with Somalia, the only shipping company that did business here was DHL, and they wouldn't ship from Somaliland to the United States. But I offered a solution that involved the College Board sending the materials to the U.S. embassy in Djibouti. I knew that the College Board didn't have a problem with that since Djibouti was already a test center. The only issue was getting the tests from Djibouti, and I volunteered to fly there to pick them up.

We were already giving the Secondary School Admission Test, which boarding schools required, and following very strict procedures. At the completion of the exam, we had to burn the tests on camera, so that the SSAT people would know we had destroyed the materials and they didn't have to worry about the contents being leaked. Still, our application to establish an SAT test center was rejected again.

From the start, Abaarso's mission included preparing students for a university education abroad, a goal that neither Somalilanders nor Americans, it seemed, could even take seriously. We did not need everyone to be accepted to college this first year, but we couldn't afford a shutout, either. This first graduating class had to make a statement, and given everything else they'd gone through, it was only fitting that they'd need tenacity to even attend the most important test of their lives.

The College Board had a position that a student should never have to cross a national border to take the SAT, but if we couldn't give a test in Somaliland, then our students would have to do exactly that. We ended up having to make two trips on two different testing dates. The majority of our students had registered for the October 2012 exam in Addis Ababa. The second, a smaller group of six students who had missed that deadline, had to travel to Ethiopia several weeks later.

The trip required multiple days of travel, using several different modes of transportation. We began by busing our kids to the Ethiopian border, where they boarded minibuses to Dire Dawa, a small city halfway between Somaliland and Addis, where they spent the night. From there, coach buses we had arranged took them the rest of the way.

For most of these students, this would be their first time visiting a foreign country. Somaliland is a conservative Muslim country. Addis Ababa, and most of Ethiopia, is overwhelmingly Christian, and this in itself would be a culture shock. Our kids saw men and women walking together, holding hands and kissing. People were drinking beer, which is illegal in Somaliland. Women were also not covered, something new for our kids of both sexes. Ethiopia also has dangerous areas, so we admonished them to stay in groups and not to wander off. We also warned them of pickpockets and thieves, neither of which are found in Hargeisa.

It was a terribly unfair position to put these kids in, having them travel to a foreign country for the first time, with the added pressure of taking an exam that literally would decide their futures. My mother reminded me of a conversation she had when driving my sister, Beth, to her junior year SAT. "How are you doing?" Mom asked. "Well," my sister answered, "considering that my entire future depends on the next three hours, I guess I'm all right." And that's how a middle-class student in the United States felt waking up in her own bed and taking the SAT in her own high school ten minutes away. And if Beth didn't do well, she could have gone back a couple of months later to take it again.

We did the best we could to soften the experience for our students, scheduling in an extra day in Addis so the kids could visit the location where the test would be administered and also get some much-needed rest. Thankfully, many of our teachers were familiar with the country. Abaarso teachers often spent their vacations in Ethiopia: it is much cheaper than Somaliland, and in Ethiopia the teachers can let their hair down, socialize, go to a nightclub, and take a break from campus life. The teachers were extremely helpful in terms of finding suitable accommodations for the students and knowing where to move about in the city.

It took a lot of coordination, including getting all the kids passports and visas. It was such an important trip for our students. Abaarso was new, so with no experience analyzing an Abaarso transcript, colleges would look extra hard at these SAT scores.

With the emphasis the College Board had placed on test "security"—that being the reason we couldn't make Abaarso a testing center—I expected there to be no cheating on this exam. Instead, I was floored by reports from our teachers of the test center's complete mismanagement of the registration. Even more shocking were reports from our students that Ethiopian students were cheating. Apparently, the test center was packed with students and desks that were nearly touching each other, a blatant violation of the testing codes, while the administrators only walked around the room to give a five-minute warning. Students in the exam were sharing answers, talking, working on answers during the short rest period between sections, and even going back to previous units after they discussed the answers with other kids during the breaks. The behavior made it clear that this center knew they could act with impunity. I was proud to hear that our students didn't participate, but I was also disgusted. We'd spent years telling them that cheating was always the wrong road, and now they had to watch others benefit from dishonesty on the most important of exams. I never wanted to send a student back there again.

Of course, I fired off a letter of complaint and again lobbied for an SAT testing center in Somaliland, this time enlisting the help of EducationUSA, the State Department's organization that promotes American education around the world. They managed to get negotiations started again, and in April 2013, it seemed the College Board was eager to collaborate with us on allowing access to the SAT by establishing a center in Hargeisa. However, to date, we still do not have the SAT in Somaliland, as the College Board rejects us for the same reasons time and again. Fortunately, the ACT (American College Testing), SAT's rival, stepped up and provided us a center. They were every bit as easy to work with as the College Board was difficult. Future students would benefit from this access, but for our first college admissions, by far the most critical, we'd be relying on results achieved under the most unfair of testing circumstances.

36

DEPORTATION

It is December 2012, nearly three and a half years since launching Abaarso, and six months since the Burao exam disaster. I have just completed my whirlwind tour of American colleges and have landed at the airport in Berbera, where I board a bus for the several-hour ride back to Abaarso. I am settling into a seat in the empty back row, when suddenly I see a soldier with an AK-47 walking up the aisle toward me. He does not speak any English. There is a man with him, someone with a uniform that indicates he is from Somaliland Immigration, and he does the talking.

"Get off this bus!" he commands me. "You must get off this bus now!" He is already having my bags removed from the top of the vehicle.

"Why?" I ask.

"You will get off this bus, and we are sending you back to your country on the next plane."

"I have a visa."

"You will get off this bus now!" he repeats.

The solider now makes an angry sound, motioning me to get up and leave. I am the only one in my row. My flight had landed in the port town of Berbera about forty minutes earlier, and while I faced some trouble with Immigration then, too, it was nothing like this. Actually, the people in Immigration seemed confused at that time, stopping me but not being sure why. I had put them on the phone with Munir, the same Abaarso supporter who helped Harry with the visas, and he'd gotten me through. But those weren't officials. They were just employees confused by their orders. The immigration officer in front of me now must be their boss, this time determined to do the job himself. The armed soldier with him should have made it that much more menacing, but I was too pissed off to care.

"I'm not leaving a place where I'm wanted, where I'm contributing a great deal, just because one or two selfish people don't want me here," I say. I then lie down on my seat, so they will understand that I am not leaving. I am not going anywhere.

"Get off the bus!" he demands.

"If you want me out of the country, then you'll have to carry me onto a plane and hold me there. If you think I'm going to help you, then you are very mistaken."

For the last two years, I have felt like a character in my favorite college book, Ayn Rand's *Atlas Shrugged*. It is the story of the movers and shakers of the world getting fed up with the abuse they are subjected to. Rand had initially titled it *The Strike* because the characters decide to do just that. They stop producing for a world that demonizes them and obstructs their progress. While I may not be a mover and shaker of the world, I think I am building something real in Somaliland. Abaarso's success, proven by our students' ability to thrive in historic American prep schools, is a true contribution to a society desperately wanting to rebuild. I am giving it everything I have, funding the school whenever necessary, working nonstop, thinking of nothing else, and calling in every favor that could possibly help.

And just as in *Atlas Shrugged*, my reward is abuse. The Ministry of Education official puts every obstacle in the way of our visas. We had to fight Khadar for the right to volunteer at Abaarso and fund the school. They tried to arrest us in Burao for administering an approved exam. Perhaps like Rand's characters, like my hero Francisco D'Anconia, I, too, should go on strike. I could leave Abaarso and watch it collapse while I start a new school over the border in Ethiopia. That way everyone can see that Khadar is a complete fraud. Is that the right move? There are certainly people who deserve that outcome, those who have behaved badly and those who have not stood up for what is right.

But there is a strong reason to fight on—the students. Not just to help their futures, but because every injustice we suffer teaches them another lesson in integrity and tenacity. My driving thought is that when they are in charge, they will not be a Khadar, nor will they be someone who watches a Khadar without stopping him. Our students are growing up to be ethical and effective leaders in a place that desperately needs them, and that is a cause worth suffering for.

By the time I was in flight to Berbera, I had already decided that Abaarso must make peace with the government. I no longer believed the government was the enemy. Khadar was the enemy. The Burao incident had been a great injustice, but I had overreacted in my response and incorrectly read it as the government not stopping until they gave Khadar the school. While I didn't know the true explanation behind what had happened in Burao, Abaarso's destruction was not in their interest. Governing in Somaliland is complicated, and where Khadar was in conflict with Abaarso, officials just didn't want to show loyalties.

Lying down on the seat of the bus, I try to focus my racing mind to solve this mess. Obviously, this government official is the pawn, but who has given the order? I am sure Khadar is behind it, but is the Ministry of Education, too? Am I wrong, and have they finally decided to give him exactly what he wants?

As soon as this trouble started, I called Harry. Harry then pulled our handful of students with influential parents out of class, so they could start making phone calls. In the meantime I wait, with no intention of going anywhere.

It is of course possible that this soldier will shoot me. I can't completely dismiss that. But I have also learned something else in my years in Somaliland. I've learned that few civil servants have real conviction about their jobs, and this is even truer for the police. This man with the AK-47 is probably paid $100 per month, not a lot of pay to engage in violence. Keeping the peace is what this country is about. Even though guns are widespread in Somaliland, people are not quick to use them. If they were then the clans would still be at war. I doubt this soldier would pull the trigger even if ordered.

"Somaliland is peaceful and wants to be recognized," I say to the immigration officer. "Do you want to be the one who shoots the American who donates his money to educate Somali children?"

My aggressors do not know what to do. They clearly have their orders, and they just as clearly have no idea how to carry them out. "Get off the bus!" one of them yells. But I am not complicit, and without my help he is lost.

Now, the other passengers on the bus get involved, and for the immigration officer and the soldier, their involvement makes matters worse. The passengers are siding with me and yelling at them to leave me alone and let me go on my way. It isn't that they are impatient, that this confrontation is delaying their travel; Somalis are the most patient people I've ever met, willing to wait hours without complaining. It is a matter of justice. They have not seen me do anything wrong, I have explained to them who I am, and they see there is no defense for the hostile actions. While the bus isn't cleared to move, the immigration officer and soldier step off to regroup and seek guidance.

Harry, meanwhile, has gotten through to the vice president of Somaliland who has gotten through to the Ministry of Interior. Immigration falls under Interior, and the ministry confirms that no order has been given to send me out of the country. The minister of education is also contacted, and she says the same. Not long after, my bags are put back on the bus, and we are cleared all the way to Hargeisa.

Shortly after getting back to Abaarso, I receive an e-mail from a relative of Khadar's whose friend was with Khadar at the time of the deportation attempt. The relative wants to make sure I am safe. The e-mail reads:

> It was Khadar who was calling the Immigration on that minute, and who told them to deport you. Be on the alert for any possible harm from his side. . . .

It continues, adding that Immigration thought Khadar was calling from an official position.

JONATHAN STARR

The witness was with him at that moment and first Khadar
declared his happiness to him, saying that he just talked to the
immigration and that you are being deported out of the country.

When Immigration called back to say the minister of education had
told them to let me go,

He became extremely mad at that news and he almost made an
accident in his car! Khadar is angry at you for exposing him, and
for showing the world who this person is. He hates me because I
supported you. . . . Work positively and change your anger into the
love for these poor kids. His cunning can no longer work. . . .
Please also use safeguarding mechanisms against him and anybody
else he may send to do harm to you, to the teachers and even to
the kids.

We had dodged yet another attack and now were beginning to see
alliances change. The relative of Khadar's who had sent the e-mail,
the vice president, the ministers, and even the passengers on the bus
have stood up to Khadar. In the deportation battle, Francisco D'Anconia's
strike has succeeded.

37

THE FULL ARSENAL

The same night as the Berbera deportation incident, the situation Khadar has created becomes dangerous. Khadar controls a newspaper that we will call *Gollis*, which he has led since I've met him. *Gollis* is based at Khadar's office and everyone considers it to be "Khadar's paper." This had actually been the source of grief for us early on because *Gollis* had been extremely critical of the government. As people then viewed Abaarso as Khadar's school, the government had in turn been unhappy with Abaarso.

After Khadar fails to have me deported, *Gollis* publishes a story that alleges that an Abaarso teacher has made comments against Islam to an Abaarso student. The article posts a photograph of the teacher who is a U.K. citizen but refers to him as an American. It also says there is a marijuana "drug culture" growing at the campus. It goes on to say that the government isn't stopping the school, so the people have to. Another news site that we'll call *Daallo* picks up the story and takes it even further. It calls the school staff Christian missionaries out to destroy Islam.

The *Gollis* and *Daallo* articles are then picked up by several other Somali news sources. In this conservative to extremist Islamic country, these statements create an extremely dangerous situation for the school. Several comments made on the websites confirm this. One comment reads, "If we kill four of the Americans, then the rest will go home." The staff at Abaarso is put on high alert.

Billeh contacts Khadar to see if he can resolve the situation. Khadar claims that he first didn't know that *his* newspaper had run the article; that whoever published it has taken it from another news site; and that he removed the article immediately upon discovering it. However, he then shows knowledge of the situation, claiming to have spoken to the family of the student making the accusation and having been provided evidence that seems to substantiate the claim. According to Khadar, the evidence can be found in a Facebook conversation between the student and the teacher accused of expressing the anti-Islamic point of view.

We know the accuser is not a student of Abaarso at all but rather a student from various other educational programs we'd been running in Hargeisa, which we will collectively refer to as the Hargeisa Programs. I had started and managed these in the fall of 2010 for two purposes: one, to provide a service to the community; and two, to have a source of funding for the Abaarso School. Just as we had not taken a new ninth-grade class after the Burao exam, we had also stopped the Hargeisa Programs, meaning our English-language program for adults, our tutoring service for grade-school children, and our college classes. However, without our permission, Khadar had opened a new office, using the same name we had used for our Hargeisa Programs. Khadar's operation recruited whomever it could from among our students, used our logos, and took credit for all we'd done while literally Photoshopping me out of the picture.

The so-called Abaarso students making the accusations are in fact Khadar's students, not Abaarso School students; it would have to be a heck of a coincidence for them to show up in his newspaper without his knowledge. Furthermore, the more inflammatory *Daallo* article appears tied to him as well. It turns out that a close relative of Khadar's owned *Daallo*, and Somalis we talked to believe that the European news site could only have gotten information about a student at Khadar's Hargeisa Programs from Khadar himself.

Attacks do not end here. We hear from our students that Khadar has sent a couple of his Hargeisa Programs students to recruit kids who had left Abaarso over the years, to help him in the attacks on us. These recruits are generally dropouts or expelled kids, and according to our own students, these kids are promised everything they want if they agree to speak out against the school and the American staff. One dropout even informs Mubarik of Khadar's offer before stepping in front of the cameras to speak out against Abaarso. With every day, the tension on campus increases. Teachers are on guard, and it is increasingly difficult to think about anything else.

Key members of the Somali community are now claiming that Khadar is trying to rally religious leaders against Abaarso. To counteract this, Abaarso plans to host a meeting on campus to show religious leaders that in fact the school is highly respectful to Islam. The leaders can watch students going about their day, observing prayer times and going to the mosque. The imams would be free to ask questions of anyone. We have nothing to hide. However, the night before the event is to take place, I receive a phone call from Somaliland's vice minister of education requesting that I delay the meeting, as Khadar is gathering the anti-Abaarso forces to create a disturbance at the campus. Harry also receives a call from the head of the police in Abaarso Village, warning him of an increased security risk due to the planned protest.

On the day the religious leaders are scheduled to come to campus, Khadar's driver comes to the gate of the school, accompanied by about twenty of Khadar's relatives from the village. They intend to disturb the planned meeting with the religious leaders, which is now canceled.

The accusations increase. Our students at American boarding schools report that their families have been told that they have been kidnapped and that I need to be stopped before I abduct more students. Fadumo writes to Harry, "I, Fadumo, and all the other kids, are disgusted with the lies people are spreading about us. Waking up this morning and seeing this just breaks our hearts." One website even runs a story picturing our students in the United States and adding them to the list of those who believe Abaarso and I are destroying Islam. The story is, of course, completely false, and I am certainly suspicious about who fabricated it.

On December 20, *Daallo* reports that Somaliland's former finance minister, Mohamed Hashi, by most accounts the most respected man in the country, is removing his daughter from the Abaarso School because of its lack of religious morality. This same story is also reported in Khadar's *Gollis*. The stories are absolutely false.

Not only has Hashi not removed his child, but two days earlier Hashi had come to the school with the parents of the girls Khadar had claimed our teacher had messaged on Facebook. The families were sorry for what was happening and upset that Khadar was using their daughters for personal gain. Mohamed Hashi was sorry, too. While it seems that the teacher had indeed written something, the families did not want to make a big deal about it and were furious that Khadar had done so without their permission. To the best I can figure it out, Khadar and his Hargeisa Programs students knew some message had been sent to the girls, but they couldn't get it directly from them. Instead, they re-created something like it, which is what they posted. In fact, when one enlarges the online image of the dialogue, it appears to show signs of tampering. It has a blurred background everywhere there is lettering, which happens with editing, indicating the Facebook conversation is a forgery.

That they have forged evidence, however, is by no means what is most upsetting about this incident. Due to the ruling of the Higher Education Commission, Khadar is at this time the chairman of Abaarso, giving him plenty of power to raise issues internally. If he is concerned about a teacher then he should bring any evidence of a possible cultural insult to me. If I fail to act then he could raise it to the entire board. Not that this would have even been necessary, as after talking to the girls and their parents we decide on our own to send the teacher home. This was partially for his own safety, but also because his actions violated our school's policy of always being respectful to the local culture and religion.

If disciplining this teacher was Khadar's goal, then such an outcome was easy to achieve internally. Instead, I didn't even find out about the situation until I read about it in the news. My only explanation for this handling, as well as all the attacks that followed, was that the Abaarso chairman aimed to discredit Abaarso and its employees, in a move that could endanger the school and its staff.

The news report about Mohamed Hashi has put the teachers in the most dangerous situation since the start of Abaarso. It is the first time I truly feel at risk. Mohamed Hashi's reputation is impeccable, his connection to the government even a big reason why people voted them into power, and if Mohamed Hashi says Abaarso is immoral, then people will believe it. At that point, even our own guards could shoot us. I take to sleeping with a baseball bat next to my bed.

Also on the afternoon of December 20, another of Khadar's close relatives holds a press conference at the hotel he owns in Hargeisa. In attendance are a few of Khadar's current Hargeisa Programs students and a couple of Abaarso School dropouts. They step before the cameras to claim that Abaarso taught Christianity and that I committed sins against Islam. The video runs that evening on two networks, Bulsho TV and Horn Cable TV. Almost all programming is paid for in Somaliland, even the news. When we asked why they ran it, we are told that Khadar has paid for the video to be played. That same day, a story accusing me of being "anti-Islam" is posted on *Gollis*, as well as *Daallo*. With the television and print press proclaiming sins, arguably a thinly veiled call for action against us, the campus is reeling. The students are devastated that their own countryman would do such a thing. One begs me, "Please go home. It is not right that you should have to suffer this."

The following day, according to officials at the Ministry of Education, Khadar visits four mosques in Hargeisa to spread the message that Abaarso employees are anti-Islam and need to be stopped. That same day, several of Khadar's Hargeisa Programs students also visit mosques claiming that members of my staff and I are committing sins against Islam. A leader at one of the mosques reportedly then tells his congregation that it needs to do something to stop the Americans. Thankfully, Mohamed Hashi steps in to speak to the imam, telling him this is a lie. Many of our male students do, too, visiting whatever mosques they can to ask where such information has come from and to explain the truth.

Mubarik writes an article for publication in defense of the school and the teachers. But the accusations do not stop, with at least one of Khadar's Hargeisa Programs students continuing to post claims on Facebook that I am a Christian missionary. Defamatory stories about me and my school continue to appear, with *Geeska Afrika*, the most widely distributed newspaper in Hargeisa, running the same news story that had appeared on *Gollis* several days earlier, in which I am called anti-Islamic. The story also alleges that our Arabic and Islamic Studies teacher, a man of Egyptian origin, has left Abaarso because the school is not religious enough. This is patently false.

Upset over the publication, an official from the Ministry of Education contacts the editor of *Geeska Afrika* and is told that a group of students from Khadar's Hargeisa Programs have approached him four times with this article, and that each time he has denied them, but it has slipped through the editorial office on his day off without his knowledge.

At Abaarso, we are now in an all-out war, not just to save the school but also to save our lives. Of all the things I imagined that could have gone wrong, it had never occurred to me that I would be accused of being a covert anti-Islamic Christian missionary, with these rumors fueled by a U.S.-educated man who had told me he wasn't religious. I could barely sleep as I worked through all the news, all our retorts, and all of the anxiety about what I'd wake up to next.

PART SIX

WINNING THE SOCIETY

Some cause happiness wherever they go;
others whenever they go.

—OSCAR WILDE

38

MISS MARPLE

Given our history of government challenges, I wouldn't normally welcome the sight of two Higher Education commissioners walking through our gates. But one look at their faces tells me the dynamics have changed. "Apologetic" isn't exactly the word to describe it, though that might also be true. Upon seeing me, their shoulders shrugged, as if to say, "Sorry. If we had known Khadar was this bad . . ."

Khadar's strategy of launching a full-on attack of Abaarso, both by trying to have me deported and by generating negative media, won him support from those who didn't know better and those who were all too happy believing the worst—some competitor schools, for example. It was a bold move that raised his prospects for a quick and decisive victory. But the strategy was also a risky one, as his true intentions would be revealed. Until this recent attack, he'd painted the Abaarso battle as Khadar versus Jonathan, which in Somaliland terms was a total mismatch. But now it wasn't Khadar versus Jonathan. It was Khadar performing a full-on assault of a Somaliland institution and everyone connected to it.

The latest attacks, particularly those in the media, could also be viewed as serious condemnations of the Somaliland government itself, as he'd implied that the government had failed to protect the society from our Western invasion. In addition, Somaliland had spent decades trying to project a reputation as being safe for foreigners. As Khadar's media attacks could incite physical violence, this was serious business that the government could not support.

In fact, the Higher Education commissioners are now on campus to clarify that they in no way support Khadar's actions. They are sorry that we are going through this, and they want to help. While the government might not yet trust me unreservedly, Khadar has unwittingly pushed us closer together.

As it would turn out, an Abaarso government alliance would form shortly after this visit, and it would come from the most unlikely of places—Minneapolis. One weekend during our college tours, Eli and I found ourselves in Minneapolis where Tom, our former math teacher, was then living. He knew some Somalis who, on my behalf, arranged an informal evening gathering for me at a local café, where I could talk about Abaarso, our mission, and our success. There were a couple of dozen Somalis in attendance, which was an excellent showing for such a casual event. My presentation was going well when someone suddenly interrupted me. "Tell us about the troubles you've dealt with," a man at one of the tables said.

I didn't know who he was, but I decided to tell it all, particularly the parts about Khadar's attempts to destroy the school. I didn't use names; I didn't even pause to consider the risk involved in speaking my mind, or maybe I just didn't care anymore. But I was ready to spill.

"I know exactly who you are talking about," the man who had opened the dialogue said. "He's a close relative of mine. . . ." *Here we go*, I thought. *Prepare for the irrational battle.*

His next comment shocked me. ". . . and I know he is a liar!" I'd be less surprised if it snowed in June.

It turned out that when Khadar had been involved in the opposition party in Somaliland, this relative had watched him behave in a scheming manner, and had even videotaped some of his bad behavior. He had then watched Khadar utterly deny the allegations. Clan loyalties run deep, but to this gentleman, there were limits. When I walked out of the café that night, the man promised to help the situation with Khadar by arranging a meeting with his cousin, an older woman who lived in

Somaliland. I was skeptical, not because I questioned his intentions but because I didn't know how his cousin could assist.

Back in Hargeisa, I am now at the cousin's gate, where a gentleman brings me to a lovely covered terrace garden, lush with potted plants and flowering vines. He shows me to the seating area, which is furnished with cushioned wicker chairs and a wicker couch. On the glass table in front of the couch, our tea is steeping and ready to be served. Then enters a spitfire of a woman dressed in a bright blue hijab.

One of my favorite literary characters is Agatha Christie's Miss Marple, the little old lady genius who solves murders while maintaining an unassuming demeanor. In *A Murder Is Announced*, she explains her method: "A policeman asking questions is open to the grave of suspicion, but an old lady asking questions is just an old lady asking questions." The not-so-old lady in the garden is Somaliland's Miss Marple, and that is how I'll refer to her.

Miss Marple's English is quite weak, though still better than my Somali, so we speak in English. I use simple words, staying completely on topic, and she understands everything because she knows all the players involved. Not that she shows her hand. She is just Miss Marple, the not-so-old lady asking questions.

She speaks to me in short phrases directly on point. She has insights and advice that, while not commands, are to be taken seriously. All of this comes with an abundance of tea and cookies her British counterpart would have enjoyed.

Many meetings follow, wherein Miss Marple heals my damaged relationship with the government. She sees Zamzam, the minister of education, a close relative and friend of hers, as the kingpin, and she masterfully works with us both until we are all in sync. My conversations with her go like this:

"No problem with ministry," she says.

"Well, I am upset because of . . ."

"No problem. Zamzam likes Abaarso. Zamzam likes Jonathan. Zamzam knows Jonathan works hard. Zamzam wants Abaarso to be good."

I'm reasonably sure she then has the same conversation with Zamzam.

"No problem with Jonathan."

"Do you know what that American did . . . ?"

"No problem. Jonathan respects Zamzam. Jonathan respects the ministry. Jonathan appreciates all Zamzam's help."

After a few of these tea and cookies sessions, I start thinking that maybe I've been unfair and the government is on our side after all. Miss Marple gets me to see all of them, especially Zamzam, in a new light. In my frustration, I'd been rash in response to what happened with the exam in Burao. I am now ready to move on, and my guess is that the government feels the same way.

Another of Miss Marple's little tricks is to invite me for tea, at which it just so happens that someone she wants me to meet is also there, such as a consultant for the Ministry of Education.

"Sit down," she says, directing me to a chair across from her surprise guest. "I check on the tea." At that point, she leaves the two of us to talk. When she comes back, she makes sure we are on the same page.

Step by step, this little lady takes two sides with deep mistrust and brings them together. It is masterfully done, without my realizing it at the time, but in the end, Abaarso and the government are on the same side. Khadar has broken what alliance he has, but it is Miss Marple who has made sure the government now partners with Abaarso.

I am told that during this time, Miss Marple is also meeting with Khadar, working her magic with him, too. Somaliland needs good schools. It doesn't need this war.

Losing the government's support is a major blow to Khadar. Without it, he has no position at Abaarso. He has taken a risk to gain a quick and decisive victory, and he hasn't succeeded. In the meantime, he's angered Somaliland's leadership, and, in doing so, damaged his own reputation.

39

RELIGIOUS COUNCIL

Of all of Khadar's miscalculations, his biggest was taking on Mohamed Hashi, the former minister of finance and a famously honest man who founded Somaliland's movement to separate from Somalia. Mohamed and his wife, Amran Ali, have been deeply involved in the school from the start, having been introduced to it by Khadar, a close relative of Mohamed's. Their daughter Suleikha is a stellar member of our charter class.

Amran and Mohamed have become major supporters of Abaarso and are particularly pleased that because of the school, Suleikha can now receive a proper high school education without going abroad. When Khadar had first ordered us to leave the country, Amran had been a leader among the parents making sure the school survived through it. Perhaps because of his close relations with Khadar, Mohamed had then stayed behind the scenes.

But after Khadar's media attacks, Mohamed spoke to the Abaarso villagers in support of the school. It was then that *Gollis* published the lie about Mohamed pulling Suleikha out of Abaarso. When Mohamed went on TV and to a newspaper with the truth, that he supported the school and his daughter remained an Abaarso student, Khadar's credibility took a tremendous hit for all to see.

Because Mohamed is a close relative of Khadar's, almost everyone who considers Khadar to be a relative considers Mohamed to be one, too. Khadar has foolishly made the Abaarso fight one in which it is Khadar versus Mohamed, which means none of their mutual clansmen has any reason to support Khadar anymore. Indeed, many now shun him.

Mohamed Hashi and Amran are by no means alone. The rest of the parents now rise to defend their children against Khadar's attacks. This is especially true of parents who see their daughters' honor under fire. They reach out to a religious council and bring the council members to the school. Religious councils are unofficial groups of religious figures whose purpose is to provide scholarly guidance. The particular group that came to Abaarso is the most respected in Hargeisa. One afternoon in January 2013, about a dozen religious scholars arrive in several cars, all of them dressed in traditional religious attire. The leader, Sheikh Mohamed, has been educated internationally and speaks English well.

Abaarso's entire student body gathers in the auditorium for the meeting with the council. The religious scholars sit up front, with the students sitting attentively in the audience. The discourse lasts for hours, during which time the council asks many questions and the students answer, explaining the truth, telling how much their teachers care for them, and all the while showing their maturity and education.

Most of the back-and-forth is in Somali. But I join in for a bit, as does Jake Galloway, an English teacher and the dean of the boys. Jake and I discuss some issues in English, which represent a bit of our point of view. When the meeting is over, Sheikh Mohamed states that the council has been extremely impressed by the high level of education at Abaarso. In addition, he notes the strong principles the school lives by. "Abaarso has better Islamic values than most of the Somali-run schools," one of the scholars declares. In fact, Sheikh Mohamed says he is interested in enrolling his daughter.

A few days later, the religious council holds a meeting at a hotel in Hargeisa to discuss their results. Parents are present, but I choose to stay behind the scenes, no longer willing to play into Khadar's story that the Abaarso conflict is really a battle between the Somali and the foreigner. The only way he can go against this group is to position himself as opposed to the parents and the religious community.

Which is not to say that I am passive. Knowing the high likelihood of a positive statement, I make sure that every major Somaliland TV station is present for the council's report. Even Radio Hargeisa attends. By the time the council finishes, much of the Somali world hears that the religious council has investigated Abaarso and has given it the thumbs-up.

While the media attacks don't stop, their target needs to be greatly narrowed as the school and the students are now off-limits. No longer can anyone claim that the environment isn't proper or that the students have been corrupted. I, however, am still fair game.

40

VINDICATION

I am asleep in the early morning of February 1 when my phone rings. I keep it near to receive word of the latest crisis, maybe bigger than the last. My heart racing, I am always ready for battle these days.

When I answer, my mind ready to problem-solve the crisis, I discover it isn't Harry with a new problem, nor is it my public relations guy with news about the latest Khadar attack. Instead, it is Nimo, updating me on her latest college news.

Despite all the time I have spent defending the school, I haven't stopped working on college admissions. Nimo's best shot is Oberlin College. I had visited Oberlin on my whirlwind tour of U.S. colleges and had seen their international admissions director a second time in New York City. I feel hopeful. Nimo is not the best academic student Abaarso has seen, but in the past year she has finally focused on her classes and the results are excellent. I implore my Oberlin contacts to see her recent grades as a true reflection of her ability. Nimo has put up quite respectable SAT scores as well, beating over half of "college-bound seniors," quite a feat for a kid with 3.5 years of real education.

I know Nimo would engage and thrive in many college activities, and who isn't looking for someone like Nimo, who is off the "involvement" chart? She has done everything possible here at Abaarso, and with passion. All students need to do four hours of community service per week. Nimo has done three times that. She is the top debater, a proctor, the organizer of competitions on campus, and a steady member of the girls' basketball team, despite having virtually no athletic talent and knowing it.

"What's going on?" I ask Nimo over the phone, hoping. Desperately hoping.

Nimo's voice is shaking. "I got in," is all she can say. She is too emotional and stunned to say more.

My clever logic student, the one who has shown the boys what a girl can do, the kid I originally knew as "the girl with the narrow face," has been accepted and will be fully funded to attend Oberlin.

I want to cry because anything less won't do this moment justice. This feels like well-deserved vindication after our struggles to survive. I have wanted this more than I can remember wanting anything. But I don't cry. I couldn't. I am still at war for Nimo's school, and there is no break until it is won. Instead, I will use Nimo's acceptance as a powerful new weapon. I just need to augment it a bit before firing.

Nimo e-mails me her admissions letter. Immediately, I call a representative of the Ministry of Education to tell him an Abaarso girl has been accepted with a full scholarship to an American college and send him the admissions letter. He is floored and says he'll tell the minister. Nimo's Oberlin acceptance breaks what has been a three-decade drought in Somalilanders getting scholarships to U.S. universities, and I tell him that I hope the minister will issue a "congratulations" for our press release.

Maybe it is Miss Marple's magic, maybe Khadar has just gone too far, or maybe I have misjudged the minister from early on. Whatever the reason, less than forty-eight hours later my contact returns with her quote:

TO: Managing Director,
Abaarso School of Science and Technology,
Abaarso, Somaliland

Sub: A Letter of Appreciation

The Ministry of Education is writing this letter as a sign of appreciation for the good news of Ms. Nimo M. Ismail for her hard and diligent work to receive full scholarship to Oberlin College, USA. This is an indicator that Abaarso School of Science and Technology is really competitive in educating Somaliland youngsters and at the same time, the knowledge offered here is accepted by International universities.

May I take this opportunity to express my thanks to the Oberlin College and Abaarso. . . . In this regard, I would welcome if more similar scholarships are offered to the girls in Somaliland in the future.

Zamzam Abdi Adan
Minister of Education & Higher Studies

With this, it is time to launch. I make sure the story runs everywhere Somalis may look, and indeed even websites we don't send it to quickly pick it up. What's more, because of the minister's quote, the papers decide to put her picture at the top of the article, inextricably connecting the minister of education to Abaarso's side. In one stroke, the damage caused by the Burao disaster is undone. Even more critically, Somalilanders know the minister's clan connection to Khadar. By congratulating the school, she has affirmed that the school is reputable, and she isn't going to play Khadar's clan games. She is now joining Mohamed Hashi, signifying that multiple big guns from Khadar's subclan are now publicly on our side.

There are several other students applying to college at the same time. On one of my trips home, I had visited Georgetown University in Washington, D.C., and they connected me with their campus in Doha, Qatar. After an excellent call with the admissions director, he invited me to a group tour of Georgetown Qatar, which is part of a series of foreign universities in Doha, collectively referred to as Education City. I jumped at the chance, since the Qatar Foundation was offering huge amounts of financial aid to all of Education City, including Northwestern, Texas A&M, Cornell, Carnegie Mellon, Virginia Commonwealth. My trip almost doesn't happen, as Immigration mysteriously, and in echoes of the past, blocks my visa extension, but Minister Zamzam steps in. I go to the conference and make important connections.

While Education City is promising, another lead that has appeared too good to be true comes through the African Leadership Academy in South Africa. At the same time that Fadumo, Mohamed, and the others were accepted to U.S. boarding schools, a boy, Hamse Mahdi, had gotten into ALA.

Hamse is an intensely intellectual student and one of the deepest thinkers to walk Abaarso's halls. Due to visa holdups, he is only now heading to Johannesburg in January, and ALA had just sent a diagnostic test for us to administer in order to determine his academic level. After receiving Hamse's test book, ALA's cofounder, Chris Bradford, sets up a call with me. Hamse's score is high and I think he wants assurance that Hamse couldn't have cheated. We have an excellent conversation, at the end of which Chris says, "You have to talk to Laura Kaub, who heads a new program we are running for the MasterCard Foundation. I'll introduce you."

In fact, I had already heard of Laura during my travels across the United States visiting American colleges. In the world of African student admissions, Laura is a bit of a legend, having done a spectacular job with ALA's college counseling. Now she had been chosen to lead a new program sponsored by the MasterCard Foundation. The program searches for high-quality sub-Saharan African students who can excel at American colleges if given the chance. The program further requires selected students to be committed to coming back to the continent, which is directly in line with Abaarso's mission. It is only for the very poor, but colleges are on board because the MasterCard Foundation is paying a partial tuition rate for each student.

Laura and I hit it off from the start of our call. She is witty and fun, but also blunt. Chris had spoken fairly when he described her as "among the world's experts in getting African students into universities." She is a pro at matching students with schools where they can succeed.

Abaarso fits the desired program in every way: our students are prepared, poor, and committed to developing their country. Laura seeks students from around Africa and there we fit, too. Neither Somaliland nor Somalia is an easy country in which to recruit.

A week or so later, Laura is using Skype to interview our applicants. Suzanne, who at that time, in addition to her teaching and orphanage work, is our college counselor, joins me in listening through the door. We may have told ourselves that listening is important to better understand our students' interviewing strengths and weaknesses, but in truth we are just too excited and nervous not to. Laura is no doubt impressed, particularly so by the last boy, whom she describes as "almost a ringer." While this sounds too good to be true and I won't believe it until I see an acceptance, this young man, Moustapha Elmi, seems on the verge of gaining an American higher education. I think back to three and a half years earlier when some of the first-year teachers didn't think he could make it at Abaarso.

In addition to promoting her own program, Laura is always happy to share her knowledge about colleges. As she says, "There's no competition among lighthouses." She has a description for almost every college out there, which often includes a witty quip.

The weeks following Nimo's acceptance pass like a dream. It seems like each day Harry and I will surprise a student with word that he or she has been accepted to college. Laura's MasterCard program places students into Trinity College, Westminster College, and United States International University in Nairobi. My Doha visit pays off when the top humanities student in the school gets accepted to Georgetown. One student is headed to Michigan State and a couple more to EARTH University in Costa Rica. After every few acceptances, we make another announcement, and with each, Somaliland begins to embrace Abaarso. And why not? Embracing Abaarso is simply embracing their own children's success. This is a clan society. Nimo and the others are their family.

41

THE CHERRY ON TOP

The staff enters the meeting hall in April 2013 with the same serious look we have worn so many times before. Our students have been through so much: school closures, attacks from their own countrymen, a visit from the Higher Education Commission, even defending themselves to the religious council. And those events account for just a fraction of the times we've gathered to discuss the latest threat to their school and their futures. Unexpected assemblies rightfully trigger fear.

I walk to the center of the stage with several other teachers wearing the outraged look our students have unfortunately come to know. Our situation has suddenly turned so joyous with all the college acceptances, and now they anxiously await what bad news could once again turn our fortunes to the negative.

I quiet them and start my announcement. "They've told all kinds of lies about us. We've had to suffer injustices and attacks from everywhere. Well, what are they going to say now that Mubarik is going to the best engineering university in the world? He's going to MIT!"

After a second of shock, the students start screaming, hugging each other, even crying. Boys and girls alike could not have been happier if they were the ones accepted. For Mubarik's victory is their victory, too. They've all fought to reach this point, and they are proud that once again Mubarik will be leading them forward. As for me, I am lost in the power of the moment. There is nothing that needs to be done now, no imminent press release, no defending the school. I finally shed some tears.

There are other victories. News of Nimo and the other female students being awarded scholarships has struck a chord with Somali women. Between colleges and boarding schools, there are six new girls headed for American private education, and many of the fanciest women in Somaliland society host a dinner to congratulate them. In attendance are our girls, our female teachers, parents, a female representative of the Higher Education Commission, and even the vice president's wife.

Nimo speaks at the event, so when our bus returns to campus I ask her how it went. "Terribly," she says. "I made them all cry."

One of the Higher Education commissioners is supposed to speak after Nimo, but she is too choked up to get the words out. Finally she says, "This is a great night. Seeing young girls so educated. So trained. Able to speak so well. Somali women have gained something so great." She compares how advanced Nimo is, her ability to deliver such a speech, to where she herself had been at that age. She congratulates all of our young women, as well as Amran and the other parents who have been fighting for the school.

One thing I hear but can't confirm is that in her emotional state the commissioner has said, "I never knew." I'd like to think she was saying, "I never knew there was so much at risk here." As Amran would say to me, before the college admissions, no one really knew what our school could accomplish. Students earning scholarships to U.S. universities had been beyond anyone's reasonable expectations. This is true not only for this commissioner, but for the Higher Education Commission and the government as a whole. I think it is true for everyone, even the parents. They have fought hard, but if they had known all that they were fighting for, they would have left even less to chance.

Billeh flies to Somaliland in June 2013 for our first graduation, staying at the Maansoor Hotel in town. It has been some time since we've seen each other, as unfortunately all of Abaarso's trouble has come between us. Billeh is a peaceful man, and I had been angry that he had taken so long to see the evil in Khadar. That is another thing that Khadar's media attacks changed. Until then, Billeh had still wanted to give him the benefit of the doubt, but after the public attacks, this was not possible. Billeh wanted nothing more to do with him.

When I walk into the Maansoor Hotel, I see Billeh standing in the lobby. My uncle is not normally a sappy guy, but he pulls me in for a hug. The bad days for Abaarso are over, and it is time for the two of us to also put them behind us.

In his short stay at the Maansoor, Billeh can see that Abaarso is now the toast of the town. We are walking out of the hotel when, coming right toward us, is Khadar's close cousin, the hotel owner who had hosted the TV bashing of Abaarso and me. He has been Khadar's most loyal supporter, even taping a video that Mohamed Hashi should stay out of Abaarso business. Now, he, too, opens his arms to give me a hug.

"We are so proud of you. We are so proud of Abaarso," he says. "And I told Khadar that, too."

We have so much to celebrate at our first graduation. We will have twenty-five students studying at colleges and boarding schools around the world, including nineteen who will be in the United States. We decide to invite parents and society leaders to campus for a celebration. Mohamed Hashi and a few members of the Higher Education Commission are among the first to arrive. We are on the same side now, the side we should have been on from the start, the side of the children. Suddenly, we hear there is a group of villagers at the gate trying to stop the event. This has been happening for months, anytime anyone comes to the school. I am told that the editor from Khadar's *Gollis* is in the village paying some guys to cause trouble.

"Well, they can't do that," one of the commissioners says, hopefully getting an even clearer idea of what we've been dealing with. He joins Mohamed in walking over to the gate. They tell the group to leave and to knock off this behavior. The group turns around, leaves, and never causes trouble again. A few dollars for qat does not buy conviction, and it isn't enough to stand up to Mohamed Hashi for a cause they don't even understand. These aren't bad guys; they are poor kids being used, and we don't hold this against them. In fact, one of them would later work for the school, making good money as a contractor.

Graduation, which includes a lot of dignitaries, opens with a speech by Nimo, and ends with Mubarik, our valedictorian—two of my heroes bookending it. Mubarik's speech is all in Somali. The crowd, which includes Somaliland's vice president, clearly are hanging on his every word. This former nomad once again shows his immense talent.

Seemingly every paper but *Gollis* covers our good news; Khadar's hypocrisy at work, Billeh happily points out. Word is that Khadar now argues that Somaliland students shouldn't go abroad for higher education, a laughable position since "I'm the PhD from America" is essentially his one claim to fame. He tries a few last-ditch attempts, including a video in which he suggests there should be an investigation into whether I have a girlfriend among the students. He pays the TV network to run the video, so it does, but nothing comes of it.

Khadar continues to run the Hargeisa Programs in a manner that looks like we are one and the same. When we change our school seal, he changes his school seal to match in color, shape, even design. When we benignly post that we are two different organizations, his organization posts that it isn't true. People continue to get confused, thinking that we are running these Hargeisa Programs; but over time, this will also catch up to him. Once anyone figures out the truth, they ask, "Why would he do that?" The look on their faces shows they've answered their own question.

The last time I laid eyes on Khadar was at a meeting that previous summer, the summer of 2012, and I am hopeful that will be true for the rest of my life. The horror he inflicted on us was traumatic, and whenever I think back to those times, I can't help but relive them. I tell one of the students that I still have this problem, my mind going back to the dark days, and my needing to remind myself that the students are okay. "We are more than okay" is her response. The roles have somewhat shifted. Now they worry about me.

Despite everything, I feel the whole experience has made me a less vindictive person. Having fought for Abaarso against so many wrongs and with so much at stake, I no longer need to fight all the small stuff. That even includes Khadar. If he cuts out the Hargeisa Programs nonsense and makes a proper public apology, then I believe I can truly forgive him. However, I'm not holding my breath.

Of course, I can only speculate about what makes Khadar finally throw in the towel. Unfortunately, here I have nothing more than speculation. Many students, parents, townsfolk, and ministers have helped us win the battle for respect and approval. But I like to think it is Miss Marple who saved the day. I've been told that she has kept good relations with Khadar for some time after, which I don't find surprising. Like a good Somali, she values peace and balance. She would not permit him to destroy a good thing, but that doesn't mean she needs to see him crushed.

PART SEVEN

WHEN ARMS
ARE OPEN

You can blow out a candle
But you can't blow out a fire
—PETER GABRIEL

42

SHOW ME THE MONEY

With our first graduation, we decide that the education would be vastly improved if students started in seventh grade. We are no longer desperate to show quick results, so in the summer of 2013, we recruit our first seventh-grade class.

Since the population is now excited about Abaarso, we try a financial experiment with the applicants. After running successful exams in both Hargeisa and Burao, we tell the high scorers that the tuition is $1,800, as that is the cost of running the school, and we can't guarantee them a spot unless they commit to the full $1,800 and send the first $300 within a couple weeks. If they can't pay that much, then they should tell us the best they can do, because there is no telling when the financial aid will run out.

By "we" telling them, it is actually little Muna who did, the still-tiny girl who'd come to us as a twelve-year-old ninth grader—the one who told me not to worry because she was taking her medicine. We still don't have local staff who can do such things, and I still don't speak Somali, so Muna is as good a choice as any. I explain the situation, then I show her the famous "Show Me the Money" scene from *Jerry Maguire* and give her the list of students to call.

One by one she makes the calls and handles the follow-ups, staying at it for a few weeks. In some cases, when we know she is talking to a top scorer, we negotiate. In others, we play hardball and make them come back with their best. When all is said and done, the results are remarkable. We have filled the seventh-grade class, only losing one student. Of course, we've made a few financial concessions, but nothing like we've previously done. Many families who originally said they could only pay a few hundred dollars now agree to pay much more and even send the money. We are bringing in the seventh grade at approximately three times the tuition of the other classes, and pretty darn close to breakeven. A couple months later, we recruit our new ninth grade, and they come in the exact same way.

An obvious question, and one I've been asked many times, is How is this possible? After all, we are dealing with one of the poorest countries in the world. The best explanation I can give is that the same clan system that had caused us so much grief is now smiling down upon us. The parents themselves aren't generally paying. But, with Abaarso's reputation, they are able to go to clan members around the world and ask for money. They just need the desire and the pressure to do so. After all, wouldn't Billeh say yes to any Musa Ismail who had the chance at such an education? Wasn't such an opportunity exactly what had given him the chance so many decades ago?

We also have Ava. Ava came as a math teacher a couple of years before but is quickly taking on administrative responsibilities. In pure brainpower, I consider her the smartest teacher we have ever had, and her college career supports the claim. She graduated from college in three years with only a rounding error away from a 4.0. As the new assistant headmaster, she makes sure our accounting is booked daily and that we budget and compare the results versus forecast. With that, she can quickly home in on any problems before they get out of control.

One significant success is our auto fuel costs, which were running well over $1,000 monthly before Ava took over. They'd increased dramatically with no reasonable explanation, but because our financial management was poor, we didn't even know it until long after the fact. Ava pinpointed the inefficiency and got fuel spending down to $500 a month, where it has stayed ever since. Needless to say, some folks had been taking advantage of us before. We were able to make similar improvements across the board, and despite a 50 percent increase in the student population, the school's operating expenses went up by only 5 percent.

In addition, Ava started properly enforcing tuition payments on all students, not asking them for more than they could pay but making sure we collect what we are supposed to. This makes another big impact on the tuition money we are taking in, which is now $200,000, versus just $72,000 the year before. On the whole, Abaarso would go from losing $182,000 in the prior year to losing under $70,000, and the path to achieving breakeven is now clear. As more students come in under the new tuition policy, and the old ones cycle out, the school will get closer and closer to covering its costs. As I write this in 2016, we are projecting the operations of Abaarso School to be within $10,000 of breaking even.

Another first for us is the acceptance of several students from the Hargeisa Orphanage, among them Rooble, a slightly built boy of thirteen, who will be a member of our first-ever seventh-grade class, and his older brother, Saeed. Rooble and Saeed are two of the students who were taught by Suzanne and her troop of volunteers, which makes their presence on campus all the more special for their elder classmates, who had once tutored them. In time, the orphanage tutoring comes full circle, with former orphanage kids like Saeed joining our crew who tutor there each week. Rooble, Saeed, and the others from the orphanage have been academically competitive while making a wonderful contribution to the school. While Abaarso must be financially sustainable, and we will continue pushing families to pay what they can, we will never stop taking society's neediest. After all, Abaarso was once carried on the back of a homeless nomad.

43

OUR BEST AMBASSADORS

The home of my friend Anand and his wife, Erica, overlooks Madison Square Park in Manhattan. The giant double-unit apartment is stunning in every respect, from its maze of rooms to its view of the city. This evening, Anand and Erica host a crowd of their friends and colleagues; their living room is packed with folks who've stopped by on their way home from work.

The world loves to hate hedge fund people, but few have ever met one or can even tell you what a hedge fund is. Those closer to that world know that if nothing else, hedge fund managers are extremely smart, and Anand is on the bright end of even this spectrum. He is a deep thinker, known for being intensely analytical, and so when he told his friends and colleagues that Abaarso was exceptional, they respected him enough to at least stop by. The one piece of analysis Anand hadn't gotten right? He's my friend who originally thought the Abaarso idea was nuts.

Today he wears jeans and cowboy boots. He and Erica thank their guests for coming. He's arranged for servers to pass around hors d'oeuvres, and the whole event seems like just another high-end party. To us, however, it is not. There is a serious goal at hand. Despite all of our success, it is unclear if we will ever be able to generate serious donor interest. As

Anand would say to me, "Why can't we be raising money for homeless dogs in Central Park?"

Unfortunately, we are finding that Abaarso is an "orphan charity," the kind without enough financial demand or interest. To the non-Somali donor, it is a theoretical concept as opposed to one that is front and center, like your child's school. The natural donor base for Abaarso is the Somali community, and while a couple of the local companies had been very generous, on the whole Somalis are not wealthy and are mostly trying to survive. What extra money they have goes to their extended families.

We haven't had luck accessing corporate money, either. Multinational companies have large charitable programs but they are generally only for places where they have offices or big consumer bases. In Africa that means the usual suspects of Kenya, Nigeria, Ghana, and South Africa. Most African countries have at least some multinationals to turn to; Somaliland has none. Greatly disappointing is that foundation funding generally doesn't work, either, though, unlike in the case of multinationals, whose explanations are quite reasonable, foundations' rejections are much harder to swallow. Time and time again we'd hear that this or that foundation just doesn't work in Somalia or Somaliland. When pushed harder, some cite the State Department travel warnings. Foundations would also tell us that we aren't scalable. They want someone working in twelve villages where in theory they could take funding and support fifty villages. That Abaarso is a completely different animal is not even a conversation starter for most.

Some experts in the fund-raising world would tell me the problem was that I was going about it wrong. But by this they did not mean changing how I attracted funds, they meant changing Abaarso into something different. With the international aid industry's spectacular history of failure, you'd think donors would want to adapt to fund what's both working and cost-effective. You'd think wrong.

Because we had been rejected by all the usual suspects, and did not have a big celebrity to hawk the cause, Anand's event was an experiment in a new strategy. We do have a few strengths, and we are trying to play to them. The first of those is that Anand, and I, to a much lesser extent, know a lot of wealthy people. Today he has gathered a room full of folks, many of whom might not notice the difference if they mistakenly added another zero to their $10,000 check. If they do agree to part with some of their money, those donations can add up quickly.

A second strength is that our product is a good one. Almost everyone here tonight has children in New York City private schools, which even for day students cost $40,000 per child annually. At Abaarso we are educating the students for $1,800 per year, and they can see from our results that the students are now on par with their own children. They can respect that.

Our real secret weapon, though, how we are hoping to separate ourselves, is that we have our products right here in the room. Everyone has heard of sponsoring an African kid for X dollars per month. Never do they say, "And then you'll meet them at their U.S. private school." We've brought five of our Abaarso students to the event to speak and then meet the guests. They are our true products and our stars. And they don't disappoint.

The first time we tried such a plan was at the Yale Club of New York City. Anand and another hedge fund supporter had arranged the gathering, which happened around the time Deqa came to America for Worcester Academy's summer school. I hadn't really prepped her for what was going to happen, nor did I think I fully could. How could I even describe a place as classy and gorgeous as the Yale Club, and the crowd of well-to-do New Yorkers who would attend? I didn't want to tell her what to say, either. I trusted her to do that on her own.

Deqa, five foot four, with flashing dark eyes, was dressed in a long and colorful traditional Somali dress, a black-and-red headscarf, and four-inch spike heels. For Deqa, the opportunity presented by Abaarso had fundamentally altered the trajectory of her life, and she let the audience know that in no uncertain terms. She didn't use words like "trajectory," but she described what her future might otherwise have been, and it was easy for the audience to imagine it. The crowd was awestruck by this teenage girl, her beaming smile, not intimidated in the slightest by the environment. That two years before she barely knew any English was beside the point, as such a speech from a private-schooled American teen would have blown people away. It was clear that Deqa was a talent who just needed opportunity. And what's more, the world needed Deqa and all those like her to have that opportunity. When Deqa finished, one woman ran up and hugged her while the rest of us wiped our eyes.

We raised tens of thousands of dollars. We also found some new long-term supporters who would help spread the Abaarso gospel. However invested Anand was before the night began, Deqa had doubled the strength of his commitment. She and the other students were the key, and now we had a whole group of them to show what Abaarso is doing.

Tonight Fadumo speaks, and like Deqa at the Yale Club, she describes how Abaarso has changed her life; her Hargeisa friends who had not gone to Abaarso were planning their weddings while she expected to study health or medicine in the United States. She would then return to Somaliland and open doors for other girls. "Fadumo stole the show" were the precise words that would later come out of guests' mouths. She was confident, yet humble. Charming, but still strong. Her words and her very presence strike a chord. And for those who'd been at the Yale Club, she proves that we aren't a one-woman show. We'd sent a different pitcher to the mound, and she is every bit as dominant as the first one.

While Fadumo's charisma would be hard to match, the night was also a coming-out party for our other student speaker, Abdisamad Adan, a short boy with John Lennon–like glasses, who had almost gone to SOS Sheikh instead of Abaarso. Halfway through the SOS/Abaarso exam, he had unchecked "Sheikh" as his first choice and changed it to "Abaarso."

Abdisamad has eighteen siblings, some illiterate. His home had no electricity or indoor plumbing, and an illiterate grandmother raised him. He excelled in his primary school, not because anyone encouraged him but because of his own self-motivation. If he needed to study by candle-light, he would. Like Mubarik, he could not afford Abaarso. He had barely been able to afford the one-dollar-a-month payment to his public school. At Abaarso, we waived his tuition, and he quickly became an academic star.

Wearing a suit that one of our supporters bought for him, Abdisamad launches into a discussion about gender. "Abaarso has changed our perception of the girls, but it also has changed the perception of the girls of themselves," he explains. "I remember the first debate we had during freshman year about whether a girl could become president or not. Every single boy and the majority of the girls said, 'No way. Are you kidding? She's a woman.' We had the same debate in my junior year after being exposed to education at Abaarso. Every girl said, 'Of course she can be president,' and the majority of the boys said yes. Only two boys said no." He smiles. "We need men and women working side by side together to transform this country into a better place for everyone. . . . The American founders wrote that everyone has the right to liberty, equality, and the pursuit of happiness. But I am sure if one of the founders walked into this room today, the first most shocking thing they would say was, 'What are these ladies doing in this room?'" He laughs out loud. His poise impresses everyone, as do his words.

Anand closes the program. In one of the most poignant lines of the evening, he points to his daughter, six-year-old Ella, who has quietly seated herself on a couch. "When I think it could be Ella with no possibilities," he begins, and it is clear he cannot let himself go there.

At the start of the evening, no one could have guessed which attendees would become the next big supporters. That is why we cast a wide but targeted net. Long after the program has ended, Mitch Golden, a financial manager, is still talking to our students. When Anand and I follow up, Mitch beams with excitement and says he will be a host for the next event. Anand's event brings in tens of thousands of dollars, but the long-term support of people like Mitch will be critical. Six months later, supporters gained from Anand's event, including Mitch, join forces to run their own event, which raises an additional $100,000. That, in turn, brings in new, long-term supporters, including Steve Kuhn, the chief investment officer of a nearly $20 billion firm. Abaarso might not be able to follow a traditional fund-raising model, but with verifiable success and our students out front, good people are stepping up to adopt our orphan charity.

44

THE FUTURE

Billeh and I are in the backseat of a Land Cruiser heading north on the road that connects Hargeisa to Berbera. In the front passenger seat is a security guard, and seated next to him at the wheel is Rashid Guled. Rashid is a Somali man in his midfifties with a bigger-than-life personality. He is fun, loves life, loves his children, and, more than anything, he loves a good story. Rashid is an engineer who received his training at SUNY Buffalo, so to distinguish him from all the other Rashids, people refer to him as "Rashid Buffalo," or simply "Buffalo." "Buffalo" now has several children at Abaarso, and he is a great parent to have on board. His engineering knowledge, in particular, has proved invaluable. He advises us and creates engineering drawings at no charge.

About twenty-two miles northeast of Hargeisa, we come to a tiny village, Diinqal, the literal meaning of which is "to slaughter a tortoise." It is thought that at some point in the village's history, a drought struck and the people had to slaughter and eat tortoises in order to survive. The name stuck.

There may only be a thousand people who live in Diinqal, and in many ways the village is just as Abaarso Village was when Billeh and I first visited—undeveloped, not much more than a truck stop along the highway. Unlike Abaarso, there is a shallow well in Diinqal that provides some water. That has led to a small but thriving orchard.

Billeh and I are looking for more land. Today Rashid has offered to help out, which explains why we are in Diinqal. We will see this small village and then head off the main road to another village twenty minutes away. This is near Rashid's tribal area, a situation I now well understand. I had told a handful of people about my desire to get land and, like everyone else, Rashid will look to whom he knows. From that handful of folks, I've been receiving offers of massive quantities of land all over the country. Some are five times bigger than Abaarso. Others are twenty times larger. One mayor came four hours from his city to make his pitch.

For several years, Somalis from all over have been pushing me to build another boarding high school like Abaarso. While I would like to do more, I fear a second high school would be a mistake. Just because something is good doesn't mean having two or more of them is better. Not everything is Starbucks.

Abaarso has dealt with Somaliland's weak higher education by catapulting our students out of the system to international universities. The actual education model, engaging students to work toward their futures, absolutely should be duplicated, not to two schools but to twenty, then two hundred, then two thousand. That is scalable. There is not, however, room to even double the amount of students sent on scholarships internationally, never mind scale beyond that. Even fifty students per year gaining scholarships abroad will be an extraordinary accomplishment.

But this doesn't mean we can't take the Abaarso education model and do more. In fact, Abaarso can be the tip of the iceberg, or, better said, the top of the pyramid. Abaarso is developing the country's future leaders, and doing so by getting them ready for the top higher education schools in the world. But those future leaders cannot do it alone. They'll need an educated class of professionals to work with and an educated population in general. That can't be done abroad. It must be done in-country.

Our plan is to build a proper higher-education institution for women in Somaliland, by establishing Barwaaqo University. *Barwaaqo* means "fertile" and "plentiful," the antonym of *abaar*, which means "drought." Barwaaqo will keep the Abaarso initiatives that can be scaled—our excellent whole-child education and our focus on fundamentals and character—while not forcing what can't—the pursuit of the international scholarships. Somali students need access to quality education in their country and Barwaaqo will provide that. Will it be a better choice than attending Worcester Academy and then going to MIT? Of course not. It can't be MIT, among other reasons because those who are graduating from Somaliland high schools aren't ready for that level of education. At least not today.

The demand for Abaarso has become overwhelming; we are now able to accept fewer than 5 percent of applicants, with the applicant pool skyrocketing each year and our classes only around fifty students each. The university will start small but hopefully reach a thousand students within ten years and double that in twenty. We are beginning exclusively with a teachers' college, so the educational impact can extend far beyond those who attend. We plan to help Abaarso students educated abroad to return to their country and set up schools that will be staffed with graduates from Barwaaqo University. I can't start dozens of schools, but our students can and I believe they will. This is their country to develop and these are their kids to educate.

The idea of starting the university came over a year ago, but I didn't want to move on it until we had the most important piece in place—our on-the-ground leader. We now have that in Ava, quite possibly the best employee Abaarso has ever had. Ava is committed to lead this endeavor. And she won't be alone, as she will have the returning graduates to join her in the coming years. In fact, she already has her first hire. After graduating Oberlin in 2017, Nimo will be right there by Ava's side. Who could be better than Nimo to lead the next generation of Somali youth?

Diinqal wouldn't become the future university site, but Billeh and I still had a nice afternoon with Rashid. It just so happened that the Habar Yoonis subclan from that area had arranged a big gathering to celebrate the opening of a nearby road. Its members came long distances from Hargeisa and elsewhere for this traditional meal. While it is not Billeh's Habar Yoonis subclan, he, too, is Habar Yoonis and several of the attendees know him. Since I have spent more than six years in the country, they know me, too.

Rashid, Billeh, and I walk to the orchard where we've been invited to join the traditional Somali meal. Mats have been placed on the ground and there must be two or three dozen men sitting down under the shade of the trees. Almost all are wearing the Somali *mawiis*, which is both cool and relaxing, a vibe that matches their sprawled-out positions. It is a feast. First goat soup comes out, poured into cups, for all those interested. Next come the giant serving platters, a couple of feet in diameter, every inch covered with rice, pasta, and cuts from a goat that was alive just two hours earlier. Everyone is in a festive mood. This is a beautiful part of the culture.

"Where are the plates?" Billeh asks.

"My uncle has been gone far too long," I tell the four others who are around our particular platter. From there, we dig in with our right hands, sharing this massive offering. It is messy, but there is also something wonderfully simple about it. We are lying in nature and eating without concerns for formalities or appearances, though as for the latter, the Somali men eating under the tree paints a great picture. Billeh looks great, too, using his left hand for a plate and his right for a fork. He is a Somalilander back in his home country and feeling at peace.

After an intensive search, we decide to locate the university in Jaleelo, a small village north of the road between Hargeisa and Berbera. Unlike Abaarso, Jaleelo is situated above a massive aquifer and, in fact, its wells serve much of Hargeisa. Because the village has plentiful water, the new Somaliland Coca-Cola bottler built its factory in Jaleelo. This, too, is a great selling point. That owner isn't from the Jaleelo clan and his factory is full of foreign workers. This means they've already worked through much of the trouble, hopefully paving an easier path for us.

The Jaleelo villagers donate a large piece of land, nine times the size of Abaarso. From the start the elders have welcomed us in. Which is not to say that everything will be simple this time, either.

At my invitation, fifteen of the Jaleelo elders come to visit Abaarso so I can meet with them, discuss issues, and make sure they understand exactly what I am planning. I have no interest in once again trusting the words of a surrogate.

One man commits to adding a piece of his land that is adjacent to the rest. The elders are happy that we will help educate the children in their town and that we plan to accept students from their secondary school into Barwaaqo. It is a very poor town with limited education. It only built a high school a few years ago, which in total only has twenty students.

I couldn't have asked for the meeting to go any better when one person in the group speaks up. He is probably a man of around sixty, his English strong. He tells me he's lived in Western Europe for many decades now. He doesn't live in Jaleelo and my sense is that he never has. He just has a clan connection to the place. Sound familiar?

He talks for a while, but his message is simple. "They say that charity starts at home, so it is suspicious when you come here." This isn't a question to be answered or a clarification he seeks. It is an attacking statement. He continues to essentially say, "This is a Muslim country and if you try to pull anything, we're going to kick you out."

When he is done, I face the group and have the translator make clear exactly what my plans are, that I have every intention of respecting the local religion, just as I've done in Abaarso, but that I am also a different person from a different culture and will do things in different ways. To them taking your shoes off can be a sign of protest. I'll probably do it because my feet are hot. I hope they can live with that. If they can't, that is okay. We'll instead go to one of the other sites where people want to host our new school.

The elders are angry with this European-Somali man for causing trouble. They assure me that they want the school and they want to work with me. Many say they don't even know who he is or who invited him.

Walking out, all I could think of is what one of the parents said to Khadar when he was preaching about our destructive Western ways. "You lived in the West for decades and married a white woman. You got educated at their schools. They were good enough for you and your family, but now that our kids are going to benefit, you say they're bad." Isn't that the truth? It isn't this man who will suffer if we don't build that university. It isn't his kids in the town who need education, and he isn't the one who has to live in that depressed village with limited opportunities and no services.

While most Africans living in the diaspora I've met are huge supporters of their homeland, I've seen this hypocrisy from others as well. That a Somaliland person who has lived in the West would promote xenophobic behavior in his poor countrymen is baffling to me. However, seeing the positive reaction of the real Jaleelo elders gives me hope that all the trouble we went through has made Somalilanders a bit more open. There are people in this country who sincerely want to move their country forward. Let's hope the real stakeholders in Somaliland welcome in the right help while keeping these particular troublemakers away.

45

IN HARVARD YARD

In August 2015, Mubarik, Abdisamad, and I are sitting in Harvard Yard waiting for the last member of our group to arrive. He has called to say he is running late, but today is so perfect that we could wait all day if necessary. All around us are returning students, many accompanied by their parents, as Harvard is now beginning its fall semester and "move-in" days are under way. Abdisamad, the boy who spoke so eloquently about gender during Anand's fund-raiser, has been here a couple of weeks already in order to participate in freshman orientation.

Being accepted to Harvard has made Abdisamad a celebrity and a Somaliland hero. One evening not long after the news broke, I was having tea with a high-ranking government official at a hotel in Hargeisa. There was a steady stream of people coming to see the official on business matters, and he made sure each one knew the news about Abdisamad. Finally, I told the official that Abdisamad would soon be at the hotel. "Can I meet him?" he asked with hope. Our boy had become a rock star. In fact, Abdisamad's acceptance to Harvard was such a big deal that the president of Somaliland invited him to the Presidential Palace, where he had then given awards to both Abdisamad and Abaarso.

While Harvard's reputation is renowned worldwide, in Africa it is considered the pinnacle of success. It wasn't that people in Africa compared it to MIT or other Ivy League schools; it was that they barely knew that the other schools existed. Mubarik was now at MIT, and I remember a conversation following his acceptance. "Congratulations on mit," one Somali said to me, rhyming "MIT" with "sit" in a single syllable. Harvard was different. *Everybody* knew Harvard.

For Somaliland, Abdisamad's accomplishment had a great patriotic value—it put Somaliland on the map, literally. CNN ran an article on its website about Abdisamad and Harvard, and the article included a map of Africa with only Somaliland labeled. All the other African countries were unmarked.

Back in Harvard Yard, our last member now approaches with a smile and a handshake. I know him well, although we have never met. He is Nicholas Kristof, the op-ed columnist for the *New York Times* and the winner of two Pulitzer Prizes in journalism. His primary topics are human rights and the effects of globalization, although he covers it all—health, politics, economics. Now that he is seated with us, passersby figure out who he is every few minutes and ask him to pose for photos, which he graciously obliges.

Do Mubarik and Abdisamad understand what is happening here? They are sitting in the most prestigious academic spot on earth, talking to one of the most prestigious journalists from the *New York Times*. Yet they seem unfazed. Nick is asking them about all sorts of things, from adapting to America, to first impressions of Abaarso, to whether they know how to milk a camel, and they are talking to him like they are seasoned panelists. Nick has to be as blown away by their poise as I am, never mind their deeply reasoned responses. I've known these boys for six years and I'm still impressed by the intellect they are bringing to each answer. With each question I get nervous for them, and then I am at ease when I realize I don't need to worry. These children are now men and they have it all under control.

A year from now, I would get more great news. This time it would be about a female student, making it that much more special. Fadumo's younger sister Nadira is accepted to Yale and Dartmouth as well as to six other colleges. She becomes the first Abaarso student to be accepted to two Ivy League universities.

As far as I know, she will be the first Somaliland woman ever to go to an Ivy League school. Back in Billeh's day, when Somalis first started coming to the United States to attend great universities, women were not among them. Yes, there are accomplished Somali women with Ivy League degrees who are also U.S. citizens or citizens of other countries. But Nadira has no citizenship other than Somaliland, and to all those young girls growing up in Hargeisa, Burao, Erigavo, and the rest of the country, she is just like them. She is an inspiration.

Nadira's success, as well as the success of the girls before her, has led to a seismic shift in what Somalilanders view as possible for their girls. Our first entrance exam with SOS had fewer than twenty girls in attendance. The most recent had four hundred. New classes at Abaarso are split evenly between the sexes, and as more of the heavily male classes graduate, Abaarso will soon be half girls, half boys. Our new university, planned as a teachers' college for women, will capitalize on all of this excitement behind female education. One Abaarso girl recently gushed that "now my sisters can have a real future."

Abaarso students, boys and girls, are convincing the world that they can compete with anyone. Mubarik, Abdisamad, Deqa, Mohamed, Nimo, and too many others to mention are the ones who made this breakthrough possible. Current and future students have them to thank.

In Nadira's case, she has another special someone to thank, her sister Fadumo. It was Fadumo who originally underwent a hunger strike to attend Abaarso, and it was Fadumo who then insisted her sister come to the school. When Nadira got to campus, she was angry and withdrawn, but Fadumo convinced her to let that anger go and strive for a future, not dwell on the past. Now, she is outgoing, warm, and appreciative. When she is accepted to her list of colleges, someone says to me, "You must be very proud." I respond with the truth. "Honestly, I was already about as proud of her as I could be," I say, much like a caring father. I had seen her actual father two days earlier, and he felt the same way.

I am proud of all my Abaarso students, not just the Ivy Leaguers and the MITs. They all have overcome steep odds just by making it through their first year at the school. Every student's success is a victory. We take nothing for granted. Neither do they.

I worry for Abaarso, Somaliland, and Somalia's future as well, but maybe I shouldn't anymore. Maybe these two men beside me, Abdisamad and Mubarik, as well as their female counterparts, will have that all under control, too.

Back in Harvard Yard, Nick turns to me. "So how does it feel to now be sitting in Harvard Yard with these boys?" I am not often at a loss for words.

EPILOGUE

Where Are They Now?

In December 2015, nearly eight years after my first visit to Somaliland, I passed the headmaster position to James Linville, my extraordinarily dedicated and capable assistant headmaster. It was time for Abaarso to have a new on-the-ground leader ready to engage in all the day-to-day struggles. James is smart, educated, and hungry, but, most important, he loves Abaarso. Before the end of his first year he told me he wanted to stay at least until the seventh grade graduated. He'll be at the helm for years to come and Abaarso is lucky for that. If and when James finally decides to do something else, my hope is that one of our alumni will be ready to take over the position.

With my headmaster duties behind me, I am now focusing on continuing the Abaarso mission, which is the long-term development of our students' homeland. Currently the biggest challenges are fund-raising, finding summer housing and internship opportunities for our students abroad, and developing our new Barwaaqo University. There is still more to do than I can possibly handle.

James has been leading Abaarso through an accreditation process with the New England Association of Schools and Colleges. The campus itself is making large strides toward the association's standards, thanks to over $1 million in grants from American Schools and Hospitals Abroad, a USAID subsidiary. Even though the campus will become much more functional, with improved utilities, a great science building, and exercise rooms, we still won't be fancy.

Admissions rates are through the roof, with over a thousand students vying for fewer than fifty spots in our seventh grade. The country is overwhelmingly behind us, and for the Abaarso teachers, it is probably hard to imagine it any other way. There are no longer any teachers who were with us during the tough times, and, as of next year, we won't have any students from that time, either. The school has advanced so much, but Abaarso cannot afford to lose its history, as that is much of what built our character. This is one reason why it is imperative that our alums come back to teach.

As of May 2016, Abaarso students have earned approximately $15 million in scholarships and financial aid, and the 2016–2017 school year will see almost ninety students studying around the world. Needless to say, my mother is stretched beyond belief trying to take care of them. Unfortunately, with these great opportunities has also come a jump in our funding needs. Our students receive extremely generous scholarships, but many of the scholarships leave out items such as travel expenses and visa costs, not to mention the unexpected issues, such as dental problems, that invariably come up. These are wonderful opportunities for Abaarso students, but with our increased numbers, we now need to raise several hundred thousand dollars per year.

Thirty-two students made it through our first class at Abaarso. At the time of this writing, twenty-seven of them have earned scholarships to higher-education institutions abroad. The students in this first group continue to be pioneers for all those who have come after.

When Mubarik took MIT's lowest-level Computer Science course, he told me, "The professor isn't teaching this from the beginning." Sure enough, when it came to technology, Mubarik had come in way behind. He hadn't seen his first computer all that long before getting to MIT, and he could have just chosen a different direction. Instead, he focused all his efforts on catching up, even skipping some other classes when he was in the middle of programming. Nor did he take any easy paths. He is majoring in computer science and electrical engineering, and when I told an MIT professor about his schedule, the professor responded that

Mubarik was taking a heavier-than-normal course load. Still, by his third year, he was getting impressive grades. It used to be that he did not understand my English. Now, I don't understand his robot lingo.

At Northfield Mount Hermon, the gymnasium includes a glassed-in display of Mohamed's athletic achievements in his years at the prep school, including his winning the Gatorade Massachusetts Boys' Cross Country Runner of the Year Award. Academically, he was also successful there, and upon graduation he matriculated at Amherst College, where he continued his all-around domination, becoming an All-American in his first year. Mohamed hopes to one day run in the Olympics for his home country, but that's not the biggest prize he's focused on. I visited him at the end of his first year at Amherst and, without my saying a word about his future, he said, "I want to ask your advice. I've been thinking about doing a master's in education because I feel like education is what my people need most." A true son of Abaarso. Here's a kid whose life has taken off, but he still owns the school's mission.

Nimo has also thrived in college, still passionate about what interests her but also making sure she gives the classroom its fair due. She is the coordinator of the Oberlin College Student Honor Committee, a student senator, an Oberlin Business Scholar, a Bonner Scholar, cochair of the African Students Association, cochair of the Muslim Students Association, and treasurer of the Oberlin College Model UN. Nimo will graduate in May 2017, and I—her proud former adviser—will be in attendance.

Fadumo went on to become an AP Scholar at Ethel Walker. In fall 2013, I took her to visit the University of Rochester, and she decided it was the place for her. The vice provost interviewed her and after the interview asked me, "Are all your students this amazing?" Academically, Fadumo remains excellent, and in terms of character, she is pure nobility. She was the one who stopped everything to translate documents for me when Abaarso School was under attack. I am sure Fadumo will stand up for justice the same way she literally stood up to speak when Abaarso's existence was at risk. One reason I know that Abaarso students will ultimately live true to their promise of building their country is that Fadumo will make sure they do.

Fadumo's sister Nadira is every bit as wonderful. She recently drove six hours in a single day to and from a New York City fund-raiser for Abaarso, and I apologized to her about the inconvenience. She looked me in the eye and said, "I'm here because of you. I'll go anywhere and do anything to help Abaarso." My mother and I were visiting her on the day she was accepted to both Yale and Dartmouth, and the normally tough Nadira even shed some tears of joy. She's now an inspiration to Somali girls everywhere.

Qadan never let her physical handicap get in the way. After a wonderful career at Abaarso, she received a MasterCard Foundation scholarship to Marist College in Poughkeepsie, New York. The summer before her freshman year, she was at a MasterCard Foundation–sponsored event at the University of Rochester, part of which I was also invited to attend. She made a presentation that included quoting back part of what I'd said to her in that conversation years before about not wasting her time wishing to be like anyone else. At Marist, Qadan earned a 4.0 GPA in her very first term.

Deqa was accepted into several great colleges, but she ultimately chose to attend Grinnell. Her optimism about life fuels her to take on every opportunity available, and at Grinnell there are lots. In March 2016, I was at a conference in D.C. for American Schools and Hospitals Abroad. Deqa came for a morning and sat with the ASHA director, an Abaarso fan no doubt, but still incredulous that our students would actually return to their homeland. After Deqa left the conference, the director came up to me and said, "I believe you now." I would have liked Deqa to stay at the event a while longer, but she was headed to her own event for the next few days . . . at the White House.

When Abdisamad took his first exam at Harvard, he thought, "Maybe I don't belong here." Then he looked around and saw a room full of freshmen crying because they couldn't do it, either. Turned out to be a false indicator, as he earned above a 3.0 in his first term and finished with a 3.5 in his second. He still expects to do better. I hope he'll be one of a long line of ethical Somaliland presidents from Abaarso.

I'm immensely proud of my advisee Amal, who also attends Marist. It took her a while, but at Abaarso she was eventually able to put the past behind her and take full responsibility for her life. In autumn 2014, when Laura Kaub, a representative from the MasterCard Foundation, visited the Abaarso campus to interview our students, she joined our girls for a game of Clue, and apparently Amal beat her while trash-talking the whole time. I believe this is what led Laura to say that our students "even curse well in English." Amal got the scholarship and has thrived at Marist. Completely on her own, she lined up an internship for the summer of 2016 at a major New York publisher. I'm hoping the young lady once known as "BBC Abaarso" will one day become a true media celebrity.

Suleikha, the daughter of Amran and Mohamed Hashi, graduated from Abaarso, spent two years at the African Leadership Academy in South Africa, and is now headed to Georgetown University's Qatar campus. She wants to be a lawyer, and I'm hoping Nimo and Suleikha will ultimately become attorney general and chief justice of Somaliland.

After Abaarso, Muna attended Choate Rosemary Hall, JFK's old school. She's been there ever since, except for a semester she spent at King's Academy in Jordan. Muna is no longer a little kid—she's grown up and capable—but she's still every bit as charming. She'll be applying to colleges in this coming 2016–2017 school year.

Fahima will also be a senior this year, in her case at Emma Willard School in Troy, New York. She's still intense—upon meeting one adult last year she launched into her full plan to fix Somaliland—but I think she's a bit more at peace with her life. Great things no doubt await her. Fahima's little brother and sister are now at Abaarso, and Nimo, Deqa, and Mohamed also have siblings in the school.

Harry moved back to the States at the end of our fourth year, but he has never *really* left Abaarso. He spent a year helping organize the U.S. foundation that supports Abaarso and then set off on a new mission, making a documentary about the school and its students. Harry has willed this project from dream to reality, and the film is currently in postproduction. He hopes to screen it in 2017.

In the middle of her third year at Abaarso, Ava knew that something was wrong with her health. Eventually, she went home to see a doctor and was diagnosed with multiple sclerosis. She came back to Somaliland anyway and stayed right up to the end of that year. Her telling the students about her condition was one of the saddest times I can remember at Abaarso, and when she left, we renamed Room 1 "Ava's Room." Once back in the States, Ava learned to handle the disease, and other than periodic flare-ups, all of which she can fight through, she doesn't let it hold her back. She landed a job on Wall Street but continues to perform all of Abaarso's accounting work in her spare time. Now, Ava has committed to lead our women's university in Somaliland. We expect this university to be the first step in allowing Somalis to receive a proper education without leaving their country. When we have the right male leader, we'll do the same thing for the boys.

After leaving Abaarso, Suzanne went to work for African Leadership Academy, where she's earned great reviews. While I haven't been able to see her as much as I'd like, we still talk. I don't know where life will take Suzanne, but she is remembered fondly by all those she's touched. Years later you'd still hear kids say, "Suzanne is my teacher."

Suzanne's boys from the orphanage who came to Abaarso made the adjustment and paved the way for more students from the orphanage to be accepted each year. Suzanne's boys are the shining example of community service at its very best and the virtuous cycle that can be created.

Many of the other former teachers continue to be connected, especially in support of our students now in the United States. Mike and Kelly are among the group who have provided housing, rides, operational help, and even gone long distances to attend our students' award ceremonies.

Billeh still lives in Brooklyn, visiting his children and grandchildren whenever the opportunity arises. He visits Somaliland periodically, and it is always in his thoughts.

The last eight years, I've been an Abaarso extremist willing to risk everything for the school I dreamed would change the country. I almost lost everything, and I went through the most horrific of experiences. Yet despite that, I wouldn't want to imagine my life without Abaarso. Everyone should, at some point, live something so consuming, so terrifying, and, in the end, so satisfying.

Abaarso's success has exorcised some of my demons, especially those that said I hadn't accomplished anything in life. With each victory, a little more of that self-imposed burden went away. I now see that my kids are on their way to success, and while I can still help them, neither they nor Abaarso *needs* me anymore. It is such a wonderful feeling to know my babies can thrive on their own.

Speaking of babies, in August 2014, I married Miriam Aframe, a wonderful woman whom I'd dated eighteen years earlier when we were both counselors at a summer camp in our mutual hometown of Worcester, Massachusetts. Then, on June 4, 2015, Orianna Starr, our baby girl, was born. Sure enough, the students posted it all over Facebook. Nimo, Amal, and Fadumo hopped on trains so they could meet Orianna before she even left the hospital for home. My daughter is lucky to have so many people who will love her like family, no questions asked. That's Somalis at their absolute best.

ACKNOWLEDGMENTS

I've talked for years about writing this book, and the only reason it actually happened was because of huge contributions from others. First and foremost, my wife, Miriam Aframe, not only took on the vast majority of parenting for our infant, Orianna, she also found time to read the manuscript, give useful comments, and put up with my having an additional obsession.

I have a brilliant professor to thank for being the first to tell me that I actually had a publishable book to write. He thought of the title and then set me up with the excellent agent Susanna Lea, who skillfully brought this project to Henry Holt. Susanna and I loved Gillian Blake, the editor, from our first meeting. Our choice was confirmed when she bluntly told me that my first draft was god-awful. Gillian and another Henry Holt editor Michael Signorelli did a great job getting me back on track. Lisa Pulitzer collaborated on this book from shortly after I signed on with Henry Holt, in particular doing a superb job of properly telling everyone's backstories. Without Lisa, I could not have done them justice.

Thank you to our students, Mubarik, Mohamed, Deqa, Fadumo, Nimo, Abdisamad, Amal, Fahima, Qadan, and others for sharing your stories with the world. Thank you to that same group for looking over the book to make sure we got it all right. Nadira, your comment that you are all "more than okay" helped pull my brain out of the depressing place writing periodically sent me. On the whole, the Abaarso students are without question the heroes of this story. Getting to brag about how great they are was a big inspiration to write it.

Thank you to all the teachers who gave up so much to join an unknown school in a tough place. Whether you know it or not, many of you provided me interesting thoughts for this book. Tom Loome reminded me that the early days were better than I remembered. Harry Lee had some particularly helpful perspectives from which to analyze the past. Ava was great in rapidly reading drafts and giving terrific feedback. She too would tell me when I was veering off.

Many Abaarso parents contributed to this book, spending hour after hour remembering the old times. Thank you for your support of Abaarso as well as this book. Amran Ali's perspective that "No one had any idea how good the school would become" was critical in my rethinking whether I'd been too hard on folks.

A grateful thank-you to the Somalis in the United States, who have embraced our students.

My personal and professional friends in the United States, the Advisory Board members, and most especially Anand Desai, have been sources of funds, advice, and connections. If Anand hadn't made Abaarso a key part of his life, we'd be nowhere near this point.

My uncle Billeh Osman was probably the only one who actually believed this dream could happen. Mom was a second editor from the beginning to the end. She and my uncle Eli Dunn also did great jobs laying out a couple of the chapters. Before I found Lisa, Eli was my collaborator. I'm sure my father would have loved to be part of it too, but sadly he died a few months before Abaarso began.

Finally, I want to thank all the people who've made Abaarso what it is. There are hundreds of you, if not thousands. It is impossible to mention everyone or even close to the number of people who deserve it, but I hope you all can enjoy this memorializing of your success. Abaarso is your school and this story is your story.

About the Author

JONATHAN STARR founded and led the private investment firm Flagg Street Capital, worked as an analyst at SAB Capital and Blavin & Company and as a research associate within the Taxable Bond Division at Fidelity Investments, and sat on the board of a publicly traded company. With a half-million-dollar donation from his personal finances, Starr created the Abaarso School in 2009. His work in Somaliland has been featured in *The New York Times*, *The Wall Street Journal*, *Bloomberg Businessweek*, CNN, and *The Christian Science Monitor*.